A WAY OUT HERE, THEY'VE GOT A NAME
FOR RAIN AND WIND, AND FIRE
THE RAIN IS TESS, THE FIRE IS JOE
AND THEY CALL THE WIND MARIAH.

MARIAH BLOWS THE STARS AROUND
AND SENDS THE CLOUDS A FLYING
MARIAH MAKES THE MOUNTAINS SOUND
LIKE FOLKS UP THERE WERE DYING.

Lerner & Lowe/Paint Your Wagon

WE HAVE NAME FOR SNOWFALL HERE
IT'S THE SPANISH WORD NEVADA
AND WHEN IT FALLS, IT'S TOUGH TO SEE
WHEN MARIAH'S BREATHING HARDER.

To Buddy

The Ghosts of Lake Tahoe
(The Stuff of Legends)

Enjoy my cottage friend

Patrick Betson

Book's Front Cover

Lake Tahoe Bierstadt, Albert (1830-1902)

Private Collection/Photo © Christie's Images/Bridgeman Art Library.

Dedication and Thanks

This book is dedicated to my wonderful mother Jean Betson, who has always had faith.

It is also dedicated to the memory of Eveline Jacobs. It is the Lord's pleasure to have taken her home but she will be sadly missed down here.

I thank the townspeople of Tahoe City who (once told) warmed up to the possibility of the book.

I thank all the various galleries, museums, historical societies, artists and individuals who have granted permission for some outstanding pieces of art and photographs to be reproduced here.

I thank Sue Twitchen for the initial proof reading.

I also thank my publisher Create Space, we got there in the end.

It would be nice to see a memorial to Hank Monk one day. If he was remembered by the greatest man of American literature, should we, the people of Tahoe and Northern Nevada, not remember him too? May I suggest a metal sculpture of a stagecoach in full flight on top of Spooner Summit?

I thank God for this humbling experience to try to do honor to a little bit of Tahoe's vibrant past.

Pat Betson

A word about the artwork and photographs in the book

Frank McCarthy paintings are some of the most stirring scenes of the Old West on canvas. His paintings are usually fluid moments of high tension set within dramatic scenery. His *"Pony Express"* could have been painted for the story of *"Solid Gold,"* the story of Tahoe's local Pony Express rider Bob Haslam.

Mian Situ is a Chinese-American artist who is still very much alive. His impressive painting *"the powder monkeys - Cape Horn - 1865,"* is a masterful depiction of what the Chinese railroad workers of the Central Pacific faced, while building the railroad through the impenetrable Sierra Nevada. The painting is a testimony not only to what they achieved but also how they achieved it. Jung Lo is one of those heroes.

Albert Bierstadt was one of the premiere landscape painters of the nineteenth century. His painting of Lake Tahoe dates from the 1860s and is featured on the front cover. It captures a sunny winter's day from the water's edge at Tahoe City and is perhaps the first ever oil painting of the lake.

Colin Bogle is a brilliant painter of natural history, his painting of the bald eagle (*Soaring Spirit*) sets one of the scenes for *"Three-Toed Island."*

Award winning photographers Jean-Louis Klein and Marie Luce Hubert are responsible for the great shot of the Grizzly bear, which is so good it is reproduced for the back cover and again in the middle of the book.

A few years back, a talented artist by the name of Michael Brent Malley did some pen-and-ink sketches for five of my stories. His skill was bound to be recognized by someone, I am just glad I got to him first. Michael went on to work for Disney; my apologies to him for being a little tardy in getting these stories finished.

Sandy Pavel is responsible for the shot of Fannette Island at Emerald Bay. She is as passionate about Tahoe, as anyone I have met. This book is written for people like Sandy who share that passion.

Finally, but not least, featured in the center of the book, is a painting of the outlet of Lake Tahoe into the Truckee river. Talented local artist Keith Brown painted this picture from a rare photograph taken before the turn of the twentieth century, I am proud to say it appears here for the very first time.

At the back of the book you will find a few historical photographs pertinent to some of these stories.

"Go west young man, and grow up with the country."
Horace Greeley 1851

The Ghosts of Lake Tahoe
(The Stuff of Legends)

Introduction

It has been said that you should compliment a lady of average looks on her beauty and a beautiful lady on her depth of character. The trouble with Lake Tahoe is that she is always complimented on her beauty but hardly ever on her character. These dozen stories will introduce you to some of the characters and heroes of Tahoe's early days, plus one or two of more recent times. Some of them knew Lake Tahoe not long after she was first settled. These were times of the old west, when nothing was faster than a horse, or a man on skis.

On a warm August day in 1876, in the beautiful lake-side hamlet of Glenbrook, halfway down on Tahoe's eastern shore, two men watched as the iron hull of the Steamer Ship *Meteor,* prepared to launch. One of the men was a Carson City newspaper reporter and the other a stagecoach driver. The two men were friends but disagreed as to the buoyancy of a hull made of iron.

"She'll not float!" said the reporter.

"I'll wager a bottle of whiskey she does and she'll serve our lake just fine!"

These prophetic words were uttered by one of the most colorful characters in Tahoe folklore, the stagecoach driver Hank Monk. His companion at Glenbrook on that summer day was the news reporter, author, and historian Sam Davis. Sam Davis was the inspiration behind the story "The Hole in the Lake." This story is of my own telling. In truth, I had never read Sam's original story *The Mystery of the Savage Sump* until just recently, but I have been relating this marvelous tale for more than thirty years. It's too good to be left out, so I hope I do Sam honor by relating my own version.

Noisily the iron hull rushed down the wooden slipway toward a very placid lake. Sam managed a shout to accept Monk's wager. "OK, you're on!"

As the iron hull hit the lake, she disappeared behind a gush of water. For a moment it looked like Sam had won the bet; it seemed she had gone directly to the bottom. Then suddenly she popped up above the spray, and as the displaced water returned to rest, there she floated as peaceful as the day. Sam begrudgingly looked at the weather-beaten face of his old friend. Monk nodded approvingly. "Don't she look purty?"

Sam knew Monk well enough to know that the question was rhetorical and the stagecoach driver was taking pleasure in having won the wager.

"You'll get your whiskey, you Greeley-buffeting old soak!"

The experience of Horace Greeley's buffeting at the hands of Hank Monk is related in "Remembering the Rough Ride of the Tribune." This story was well known during the latter half of the nineteenth century, it has been long since neglected, so here I try to tell it afresh. Again, I hope I do Hank Monk and even Horace Greeley justice.

The friends of that summer's day in 1876, Sam Davis and Hank Monk, are both buried in Carson City's Lone Mountain Cemetery. After sixty years of faithful service, the SS *Meteor* was purposely sunk in 1939, and it now rests on the bottom of the lake in several hundred feet of water. For years she towed cut timber from the south and west shores of the lake to the saw mills of the Carson Tahoe Lumber and Fluming Company at Glenbrook. After the timber-cutting years, she served as a mail delivery ship and passenger cruiser and out-lived both Davis and Monk. Her sister ship, the Steamer Ship *Tahoe* launched in 1896, was sunk in 1940, a year after the SS *Meteor*. The SS *Tahoe* lies just off of Glenbrook Bay in about four hundred feet of water.

Captain Dick Barter (featured in Three-Toed Island) is also buried somewhere in the depths of Lake Tahoe. Pony Bob Haslam (Solid Gold) is buried in Chicago. Mark Twain (The Immortal Faces Death) is buried in Elmira, New York.

Our bad man Jim Stewart (The Dreaded Evening Drink) is buried in Tahoe City's Trails End Cemetery. The final resting place of Martin Lowe (From Disaster to Triumph) is unknown. Snowshoe Thompson (Sesquicentennial) is buried in Genoa's Cemetery. Jung Lo the Chinese railroad worker (Jung Lo) never existed, but thousands just like him did. A few of them fell to their deaths or were buried in avalanches and rock slides, never to be recovered. Col Claire and William Meeker still live in our imagination. The chef and lady friend (Mutiny at the Inn) are buried in Switzerland (but not together,) and the waiter is buried in Glendale, California. Alex Cushing (In the Halls of Zeus) died in Newport, Rhode Island, in 2006. Old Ben (The End of an Era) does not lay at rest but still flies above us all.

For a moment, I am raising the others from their resting places, and we will know them again briefly. The characters, heroes, and villains of these stories are mostly men, but the true star of this book is the beautiful lady whom these men either came to visit, or came to call home. She is a beauty, but Tahoe really does deserve more than just your wolf whistle!

First and foremost, this is a book of twelve short stories and not a history book, but some background will (I hope) help the reader enjoy the stories even more. Therefore, every story has its own historical background with postscripts.

Here, then, are The Ghosts of Lake Tahoe!

"I know a man who went there to die but he made a failure of it!"

Mark Twain, 1872

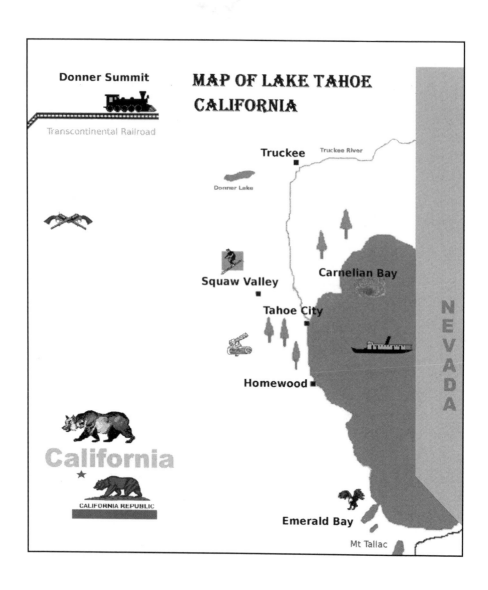

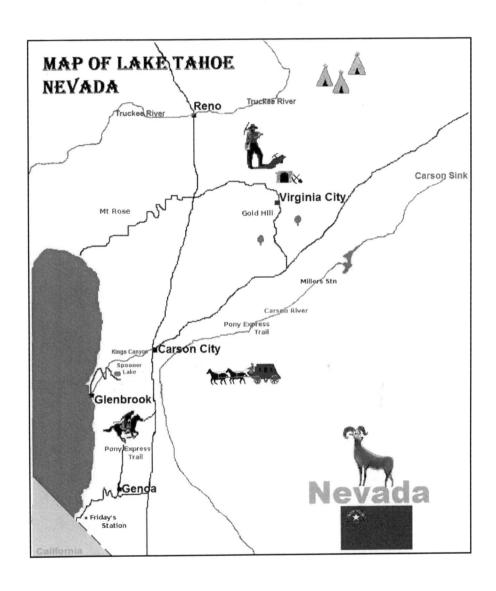

Table of Contents

1) Solid Gold, 1860

It was a blustery early June night in 1860. Outside the forge, the wind slapped the trees as the dark clouds rushed overhead. Despite the lateness of the year, wintry weather was obstinately hanging on, but the pine pollen, already thick in the air, indicated that summer was being held back against its will.

Inside the forge, the stranger watched as the blacksmith used the long tongs to grab a crucible from the furnace. The smithy poured the molten metal over a crudely shaped rock inside a tin can.

"Before the gold completely cools we'll pull the rock out, so it won't stick unevenly. Then you'll have one cheap golden nugget and one expensive tin can!" The smithy laughed at his own humor, but the stranger didn't smile. "Mind you, your nugget won't fool anyone who knows gold."

"It's only supposed to fool the masses," quipped the man in response.

The tents and shacks of the Forty-Niners had long since disappeared. Towns had been planned, with Victorian houses, gardens, schools, banks, and merchant stores. It should have been a developer's dream, except there were no new people. The excitement of the Gold Rush was over; the dream of statehood was a reality. Farmers were coming to California

1

but were settling in the valleys. A large movement of prospectors was now headed east out of California to the silver mines of the Washoe Hills. No one was stopping in the foothills above the Sacramento valley, where the stranger had invested thousands of dollars. There was nothing to attract emigrants to stay. Maybe a rumor of a new gold discovery might help. And to start a rumor, you need a starting place.

A few days later, the stranger boarded the Lake Tahoe-bound stage at Hangtown on a bright summer's morning. The plan was simple enough, but first he had to leave the immediate area, where he was known. Since the massacre of seventy-six men near Pyramid Lake to the north of the Comstock silver mines, there were daily horror stories of Paiute Indian attacks along the Carson River. The fearful stranger did not want nor need to go beyond Lake Tahoe. Many silver miners would stop at the growing community on Tahoe's south-east shore for rest and supplies, before heading up and over to the silver mines forty miles to the north east. The fake nugget had to make it east, but because of the Indian attacks the stage was often not running beyond Carson City.

The Pony Express was the only alternative to the stage. On its way east out of California, the Pony Express ran nearly two thousand miles from Sacramento to St. Joseph, in Missouri. Barely a hundred miles out of Sacramento, the Pony Express ran around the south shore of Lake Tahoe, and went up and over the eastern range of the Sierras. The Pony Express usually only carried letters and dispatches, at a cost of five dollars per ounce. It was not cheap but was considered good value, provided it got through.

Young lightweight riders covered an average distance of sixty to seventy miles apiece over four or five stations, with a change of pony at every station. Each station would keep an eye out for an approaching rider. At an interim station, a new mount would be waiting. The young rider would jump off and, without pausing, jump onto his new mount. Upon reaching his last station, the young rider would pass the service mochila to the waiting hands of a new rider. The new rider, already mounted, would take the mochila and fix it to his saddle and be into a hard gallop out of the station in less than two minutes.

To convince the Express to take his nugget was a challenge for the man, but he felt the nugget's existence would start loose tongues talking right along the chain of stations. Having reached the Tahoe community, the stranger asked for directions. He was told Fridays Station was five miles to the north of town. The stranger chose to walk rather than hitch a ride with a sympathetic silver miner. A lot of silver miners had been gold prospectors before, and they were a little too savvy for the man's liking. The less other people knew about his intentions, the better it would be. He had no need for small talk or friendly questions that he might have to deflect.

Annoyed and a little thirsty, the man arrived at Fridays Station. The newly built station was made of white weatherboard and someone had attempted to create a garden, with a few colored flowers surrounding a grassy patch under the shade of some Ponderosa pines. There were pony noises coming from the stables beyond, but no human activity was evident from the outside. So the stranger pushed open a side door of the main building. He came across a young lad sleeping awkwardly on a table. The lad's head hung backwards off the edge of one end, while his feet were propped up on the sill of an open window. He had one arm by his side while the other arm dangled with his knuckles scraping the floor. It might have been a natural repose for a drunkard, but the lad did not drink; he was just exhausted.

Young Bob Haslam had arrived unexpectedly at Friday's, just before dawn. Tyler, his relief rider, had to be woken up from a deep sleep before the dispatches were taken further west. During daylight hours exchanges were immediate but sometimes during the night things did not go quite as smoothly, especially when it was a change of riders. Ted, the stationmaster, had told everyone at the station not to disturb Bob's sleep. So the young lad had been left in his precarious position on the table, to sleep the day away if necessary. The traveler, however, had little sympathy and since Bob did not wake at his first request, he started to prod the lad. "Wake up boy," the man demanded.

Bob slowly opened one eye, as his left hand came up to rub the other. Sleepily, trying to regain consciousness, he peered at the intruder before him. His first utterance was a polite "Yes, sir?"

The stranger was irritated. "Is there no one with any authority here?"

"Ted is sure to be around somewhere, sir." Bob had swung his legs over the side of the table and was now sitting upright.

"Well, why don't you do something useful and find him for me?" the newcomer sneered.

Ted was eventually found, though he was none too impressed by the man's off-handed manner. He was even less impressed when the stranger told him of his purpose. Ted looked at the gold-covered rock, raised an eyebrow, and knew something was not right. "The Express does not deliver cargo," he emphatically told the man.

"It's hardly cargo," countered the stranger. "It weighs less than nine ounces, and it's imperative that it reaches St. Louis by the quickest means possible."

"You'll have to wait for the stage, then." Ted turned as if to end the conversation.

The man felt a sudden rush of blood to his face but forced himself to be pleasant. "Since the stage is not running at present, I will be glad to pay whatever price you deem necessary for accommodating me."

"One hundred dollars!" Ted hated to be bought but he was not going to be bought cheap.

The stranger's eyes narrowed as he looked hard at the station master. Begrudgingly, he accepted. "OK, one hundred dollars and you will take it east to St. Joe?"

"Yes, but there won't be a ride east for a couple of days and the service is not responsible for any loss, damage, or theft."

Having filled in the necessary paperwork and paid more than twice the going rate, the man left Fridays Station never to be seen again.

Bob was fast becoming a favorite with everyone in the service. He had one of the most difficult rides to cover between his two home stations. Bucklands, in the east, and Friday's, in the west, were a good seventy miles apart. The two stations could not have been more different. Bucklands was in the parched desert surrounded, by a few hills covered in sage brush and ten-foot Piñon pine trees. Friday's stood close to Lake Tahoe's southeast shore and was surrounded by snow-capped mountains with huge Ponderosa pines and tall cedar trees. Despite Lake Tahoe's grander scenery, Bob enjoyed Bucklands as much as Fridays. The hills surrounding Buck-lands were home to many wild horses. On his days off, Bob went on mustang round-ups to find new ponies for the Serv-ice. He would get paid for every new pony he corralled and extra pay if he was responsible for breaking a pony in.

The ride east of Dayton through the Honey Lake Valley to the Carson Sink was the most likely for Paiute attacks, and Bucklands was in the heart of this dangerous stretch. Despite recent attacks, the Pony Express had continued to ride, but it was now a company edict that every rider had to be armed. Bob quickly learnt how to handle a Colt revolver and a Spen-cer rifle, but using a gun was always considered a last resort. A Pony Express rider was meant to outride any trouble by putting as much distance between him-self and any danger.

A couple of days after the stranger had left; Bob was ready for his ride east. The warm day at the lake meant it was going to be a hot one down in the valley. With his mount Grummer tied to a fence, Bob sat on a bench underneath the shade of some pine trees. The first leg out of Fridays going east was up the Kingsbury Grade over Daggett Pass. The ride was punish-ing for any pony, with a two-thousand-foot climb and then a four-thousand-foot drop down into the Carson Valley. It was the most arduous leg on Bob's route, but it was perhaps the least likely to be attacked by Indians. Grummer was a bay colt, a little bigger than the other ponies. Although not the fast-est horse, he was strong, and he was the first choice for the Kingsbury Grade, which needed a sure-footed horse of character. Grummer's stamina was even more important on the way back to Fridays, riding west from the Carson Valley, when the climb was twice as high.

Bob was waiting for Tyler's return; Tyler rode between Friday's and Webster's Station on California's American River. On his ride east out of Webster's, Tyler had arguably the most beautiful ride of any rider in the service. Lake Tahoe was always a glorious sight as he rounded Echo Summit. He had never envied Bob riding the desert east beyond the Sierras, even less so with the current Indian troubles. As much as Tyler enjoyed his ride, he looked forward to arriving at Friday's, where there was always a good meal waiting. This day he was particularly hungry, so he rode furiously down from the summit and along the Lake's southern shoreline.

On a warm, dusty day, an eastbound rider out of California could always be seen a few miles off. The stationmaster's office window faced south and it looked straight down the approaching road. Ted shouted down to Bob that he thought Tyler was about ten minutes out. Bob mounted Grummer and was ready as Tyler burst into Friday's courtyard. With a cheery exchange, Tyler threw down the mochila into Ted's waiting arms. Ted extracted the enclosed dispatches and sorted through them quickly. Satisfied that none were for his own personal attention, he added the few which were in his care, along with the nugget left by the stranger. Having strapped the mochila closed, he tossed it up to Bob.

Bob was already into a canter before he shouted his farewell. The ride with Grummer and his other mounts, through the Carson and Eagle Valleys, were pretty uneventful. The day had become noticeably stickier as the temperature rose. Having mounted his fourth horse at Dayton, Bob rode upward to his next stop, Millers Station. As Bob came over the rise, a pall of black smoke was distinguishable on the horizon. For a month Indians had attacked stations and set fire to remote cabins up and down the Carson River. A sudden sense of urgency gripped him. Miller's Station was now a visible speck but still more than five miles away. Turning back was not an option; his only thought was getting to Miller's as quickly as possible. His mount out of Dayton was a chestnut filly, and she responded to his encouragement as they sped down toward the distant station.

To his left, on the far side of some Piñon pines, Bob became aware of some swirling dust. It could have been a small dust twister or a small group of mustangs; regrettably, it was neither. It was four piebald ponies ridden at full gallop by four Paiutes. It was going to be a race. Although the Indians were no more than two hundred yards to Bob's left, there were many Piñon pines between him and his pursuers. By the time they could have joined the trail, Bob should have gained some valuable distance. But now was the time, before they came from behind to try a shot or two. Raising his six-gun, Bob fired off three rounds. He hit one of the ponies and as it stumbled an Indian was unceremoniously thrown over his pony's head.

Two Indians were making for the trail, but the third tried his best to keep a parallel course. It was a masterful piece of riding. The Indian swerved and careened around every onrushing Piñon pine. Despite the trees, the Paiute was seemingly closer. Bob fired again, a shot that must have gone close over the piebald's neck, but there was no perceptible slowing of the Indian's progress. A second shot hit one of the Piñon pines and a shower of pine needles momentarily flew around the Paiute's face. Bob loved horses, but in a case like this, the pony made a better target than its rider. Holding as steady as he could, with the chestnut pounding the ground beneath her, Bob fired once more. The Indian pony was hit in the flank; it skidded through the dust, taking large clumps of sage as it went. The unseated warrior was able to hang onto the neck of his badly wounded animal, but his chase was over.

There was no way to reload and there were still two Indians in hot pursuit. With horror, Bob realized, in his fierce determination to get an accurate shot off, that he was no longer riding the trail. Somehow the chestnut filly had headed into the brush and was no longer on a straight course for Miller's Station, where the only conceivable help might be. Bob could not now change course without lessening the distance between himself and his murderous foe. His enemies were gaining ground, his pony seemed measurably slower, and desperation started to flood the young rider's senses. His chest ached with each pounding heartbeat, while his clenched fingers feverishly shook his will for greater haste through the reins. In sudden terror, Bob became aware that at least one of his would-be assassins was whooping his unintelligible cries within earshot.

As his mind raced, Bob felt reality slow down; every second seemed an indeterminable amount of time. In slow motion he was aware of a piebald pony next to his chestnut filly. He sensed a tomahawk above his head. With sudden dexterity Bob threw his empty six-gun at the Indian's face. The Indian's expression changed from murderous intent to one of anguish, but he managed to duck as the empty gun barely missed its target. Bob had bought himself a few extra seconds as their two ponies momentarily drifted apart. The Indian recovered his lost momentum and was again on course to deliver a decisive blow.

Bob was desperate for any kind of weapon. His hand fumbled around his saddle and he touched something hard inside the mochila. The tomahawk came crashing down but Bob was able to avoid its full force by throwing his body forward. The blow hit him on the top of his left arm. The Paiute went to strike again but instead of bringing the tomahawk down, the Indian crashed to floor. The Paiute was now lying in the dirt; a throbbing pain tore through his head and blood filled his nostrils. Bob had managed to open the mochila and grab the hard object. Hurling it straight, he had hit the leering face just above the eye. The Indian had toppled like a coconut shy and the rider-less piebald pony was now running off into the desert.

The fourth Indian rode past his fallen comrade. He, too, was now gaining ground. Bob chanced a look backward, and the warrior was no more than fifty feet behind. Bob now had nothing to use as a weapon. It would take a miracle to escape. The chestnut was still pounding the ground but the gap between the two riders was closing rapidly. A piece of Piñon pine debris flew off a nearby tree. Bob was unsure at first, but there it was again, an audible "WIZ-ZZZ." Someone was firing a rifle from a now much nearer Miller's Station. Taking a chance on it being friendly fire, Bob jerked his chestnut at a right angle. At the instant the pursuing Indian realized what was happening, it was too late. One bullet hit him in the shoulder and a second hit him in the chest.

With constant threat of Indian attack, everyone at Miller's was in a heightened state of nervousness and a constant vigil was being kept. The stationmaster, Abe, had watched the approaching dust cloud from the southwest. He had realized it might be a white man in trouble. At first it was too far to discern, but after a short time it was clear that a lone rider was being pursued by a number of Indians. Abe had aimed his rifle, waiting for them to come into range. For a while it was too risky, the fear of hitting the lone rider made him wait. But it looked like a pretty desperate situation, so he chanced a couple of shots. Then, suddenly, he had a clear shot and wasted no time bringing the Indian down.

Out in the brush, a mile or so from Miller's station, an Indian with blood in his eye sat upright in the dirt. He was looking at what had knocked him from his pony. It was a shiny yellow rock! The Indian picked it up and threw it with disgust into the sage.

 *(2) The End of an Era, 1862*

Old Ben awoke to a dull pain in his right shoulder. The bullet was still lodged there, but the burning sensation had passed. His assailant was dead. The attack had been unprovoked.

He had walked into a prospector's camp late at night in the hopes of sharing a meal and the warmth of the camp fire. The prospector, who had been less than friendly, went for his gun. Despite being quick, Old Ben was quicker. The prospector was dead and Old Ben was only wounded.

He had lived in the Sierra Mountains long before the Comstock bonanza of Virginia City. He had known them as a haven of tranquility, but now his solitude was disturbed by an endless stream of wagons and horses. He had known when the fish were plentiful in the shallows of Lake Tahoe. The fishing had been easy but now there were too many fishermen. He had lived among the Indians with no trouble. However, these silver miners were gun-happy, they had no respect. He had been forced to kill a dozen of them.

Old Ben had slept the night in the camp, after eating the prospector's rations. The ground was moist and his coat was damp. He needed to leave the shade of the trees to find the warm morning sun. He walked towards the steep mountain road, which would take him back over to the lake. Upon reaching the road, his sudden appearance so startled the horses of an oncoming wagon that they reared in fright. The road was narrow. One horse lost its footing and slipped, and the wagon overturned. The wagon, horses, and occupants somersaulted down the steep slope, hundreds of feet, until the wagon broke against the pine trees. It was unlikely that any man or animal could have survived such a fall. Anyway, Old Ben cared not; he was more concerned with finding warmth.

As he reached the top of the road the sun greeted him, and beautiful Lake Tahoe lay at his feet. A group of men, who had stopped near the top of the road, were also enjoying the sight.

"GRIZZLY!" shouted a fear-filled voice.

The firing of half-a-dozen guns echoed among the granite boulders. The big creature fell backwards. Its bellowed moan continuing for several seconds till it became faint. The lips stiffened, the tongue lolled to one side, and the eyes in its huge head grew dull and glassy, life gently slipped away and was gone. Old Ben was dead!

3) The Immortal Faces Death, 1863

Mark Twain spent a sleepless night. He had written a will, leaving what few belongings he possessed to his brother Orion. His dictionary he had left to his friend Steve Gillis.

Steve Gillis was Mark's confidant, work colleague and friend. There was one honor a friend could achieve beyond being asked to be the best man at a wedding, and that was to be their chosen second in an affair of honor. Fighting a duel and getting married may be considered identical by many, but a duel had one advantage over marriage brevity! Unfortunately, it was the permanent state of death that bothered Mark through his sleepless night. He had been deliberately carefree throughout his young life, and now it was so damn serious. How had it changed so dramatically and in so short a time?

He had loved being a reporter at *The Territorial Enterprise* in Virginia City. Exciting news sold newspapers; the truth was often dull and boring. You had to give the public what the public wanted; a little bit of scandal, some controversy, veiled innuendos, veiled accusations, stories of betrayal, and tales of corruption. It was in these areas that a great reporter shone with inventive intrigue and inspired imagination. A lack of originality was a virtue of an undertaker, but a reporter had to aspire to give a story life so there would be no need for an undertaker or indeed burial.

What had he done, that was so awful? He had posed a question as to the honesty of some of the ladies of the Women Institute in Carson City. It had been a question, just a mere suggestion, concerning the handling of their financial dealings. No direct accusation, no individual singled out. It was tame in comparison to some of his past work. After a brief outrage, it should have been forgotten but for some reason *The Daily Union*, the opposing paper in Virginia City, had sought to make an issue out of it. Their reporter, James Laird, had written a rebuttal directly accusing Twain of lying, and calling the Enterprise a rag of deceit. It was certainly a lack of originality when you had nothing more inventive than to accuse your rival newspaper of not telling the truth. *The Daily Union* could take the moral high ground, but they would never sell more newspapers!

The stupidest thing about a duel, besides getting yourself killed, was all you had to do was win it and you were vindicated. It did not matter how much in the wrong you might be; if you were the victor, to you went the absolution. This seemed to Mark more of a distortion of the truth than any story he could ever invent. However, honor had to be preserved.

It was all too civilized; an appointment at dawn; a pair of dueling pistols firing one shot apiece; two gentlemen seconds above reproach to ensure that the rules of engagement were not tampered with. Gentlemen never fought on a street in broad daylight or in the view of bystanders. They went to a remote location at a time when there would be no innocents abroad. A killing of an adversary in a duel was never considered murder; it was the simple upholding of honor. Whatever the outcome, after both parties had discharged their weapons, the result would be accepted and no reprisals were to be sought on either side.

Still, it was all stupidity to Mark, who had come out west with his older brother three years earlier. On their journey, which had been mostly by stage, Mark had carried an aging derringer that he had feared to fire, just in case it malfunctioned. He was not used to firearms and indeed had never fired one. Now he needed some practice, otherwise he was going to face certain death, unless his opponent was going to miss too! He thought of approaching his opponent of the Daily Union and suggesting that they agree to deliberately miss each other. Still, Mark did not know if he could miss on purpose and feared he might kill Laird by accident! It was also a risk trusting Laird to agree to such an arrangement; if he refused he could hold Mark up to ridicule.

"I'm committing suicide," he had told Steve. "What do I know of fighting duels?"

"It's a great honor, Sam," Steve had replied, calling Twain by his given name. "You're fighting for the glory of the Enterprise."

"And the demise of yours truly!" Twain had countered. "I understand Laird doesn't want to fight the duel either, so why are we pursuing this folly?"

"Because of Joe." Steve ended the conversation on those three words. The words continued to run through Twain's mind, as he tossed and turned in bed.

Joe Goodman was the editor of *The Territorial Enterprise*. He had flown into an unholy rage when he had seen the rebuke in *The Daily Union*. Initially, Mark had tried to placate Joe by saying that he was not much insulted. Mark watched Joe turn several shades of purple and every vein in his head bulge as he told his star reporter that he did not care that Mark was not much insulted. It was the paper that had been insulted, the editor who had been insulted, everyone associated with the paper that had been insulted. Joe demanded an immediate apology to be printed on the Union's front page and everyone was on tenterhooks while they waited for the Union's response. A messenger boy arrived at the Enterprise workshop with a note from the Union's editor addressed to Joe Goodman. Unopened, it had been taken up to Joe's office on the second floor above the workshop.

Joe called Mark up to his office, and had him sit down. "Grim news for you!" he said as he handed the delivered note to Mark. The note was brief, unsigned, and to the point. It read "No apology and no retraction!" Mark looked up from the note and at his editor, not knowing how these events would play out. He looked for some clue on Joe's face, but his editor was expressionless. "Nothing left for it Mark."

Still, not quite following his editor's lead, Mark shifted uneasily in his chair and asked what Joe intended to do. The answer was like a thunderbolt!

"We shall all stand behind you. You as a loyal member of the Enterprise staff shall demand satisfaction of the scoundrel, who called you a liar and besmirched the greatest newspaper in the territory!"

The news filtered through to the boys in the workshop, and as Mark came down the stairs, every employee gathered to greet him. Some of his fellow workers clapped, and others rushed to shake his hand, or slap him on the back. For a moment, he was a hero........., a very reluctant and worried hero!

Mark Twain had been a hapless witness as the demand for satisfaction had been composed; all he was asked to do was to sign it. He was now being swept along by the euphoria of others. At the Union paper they were expecting a messenger boy to deliver some form of reply. However, the Enterprise had upped the stakes. It was Goodman's idea for Steve Gillis to deliver the demand for satisfaction to James Laird in front of the Union editor and for Steve to inquire who Laird's second would be. Steve's reputation with a gun was well known, and the knowledge that he would be Mark's chosen second added an air of defiance to the demand. The Enterprise had pushed the rival newspaper into an inescapable corner; it was either total capitulation or see the matter through to the bitter end. James Laird was of the mind to apologize, but he could tell it was already too late.

It was all set. The demand for satisfaction had been accepted. The duel would take place an hour after sunrise at the base of Gold Hill, the day after tomorrow. Steve had met with Laird's second and the weapons were chosen. A doctor was to be in attendance, and his services were to be paid by the Enterprise. Despite the interest of employees from both papers, Mark had requested that there would be no additional persons to be present.

Steve could feel Mark's apprehension and tried his best to encourage his friend. He told Twain that they would get up early and take some target practice before the appointed hour. This did nothing to calm Twain's nerves and he knew he would not sleep a wink for the next two nights!

Mark was forgiven for not working the next day. He went around in a trance unable to focus, nor give any thought to anything outside his impending doom. He thought about visiting his brother in Carson City, but the temptation not to come back would have been too strong. Everyone at the Enterprise was exuberant, greeting him with more affection than he had experienced at any time over the past three years. He greeted their cheery faces with a weak, forced smile. He felt this odious weight of duty, and he vowed if he should, by some miracle, survive tomorrow's ordeal then he would leave Virginia City for good.

There had been good times, especially when Artemus Ward had come to visit. He wondered how Artemus would have handled a similar situation. He imagined Artemus holding onto his lapels and saying, "When reality doesn't add up to much, pretend you're hiding something. Sow the seeds of doubt!"

However, Mark was too busy pretending he wasn't scared, to pretend he was quietly confident.

Steve Gillis was the only person who really knew Mark's state of mind, and he was determined to allay his friend's fears. He went round to Mark's dwelling early on the morning of the duel, while it was still dark. Mark was lying on his bed, fully clothed; he had watched the flickering oil lamp dance upon the ceiling for hours. His mind was now resigned, which relieved the constant mental anguish of planning some escape. He did not know his opponent Laird well, which was probably a blessing, but he could not remember ever seeing Laird with a gun. That might indicate that he too was not used to firearms. He had determined to let Laird fire the first shot. If Laird missed, then he would miss too, on purpose (if he could!)

"Sam, are you ready?" Mark jumped, even though Steve's voice was barely a whisper.

As Mark opened the door he said with some indifference, "Is anyone ever ready to die, Steve?"

Steve walked into the room and looked hard at his friend in the flickering light. "Enough of that Sam, you are not going to die. I won't let you."

Mark managed a small smile; his friend's words smacked of sincerity. Steve's confidence was what he needed now above all else.

"I told you we would have some target practice. I spent two bits on a watermelon and it will make a fine target. There's Hampton's barn on the edge of town just before Gold Hill, and we'll place the watermelon on top of the barn door. I've got my service revolver, my Colt 45, and plenty of bullets."

The early morning air was cold as they arrived at Hampton's barn, the pale light of dawn just visible above the distant hills in the east. Gillis placed the watermelon on top of the door of the disused barn. He had Mark stand some thirty paces away and went through the basics of aiming and firing a weapon. Mark thought he had a pretty good idea of the basics, but felt he was a little unknowing on the finer details. Steve emphasized that a duel was not like a gunfight. Quite often a gunfight depended on who fired the quickest. A duel was a more measured affair. In a gunfight, a gun might be fired from the hip; in a duel, one had to aim, by raising the pistol with an extended arm and to look along the barrel. It was important to be deliberate: a dueling pistol fired in haste often resulted in missing the target and then having to suffer an excruciating wait while your opponent took his time. Neither protagonist was allowed to move until both firearms were discharged.

Standing shoulder to shoulder, Steve Gillis gave his service revolver to Mark. In effortless fashion, Steve pulled out his Colt 45 from its holster and shot a hole, straight through the center of the watermelon. Mark was dumfounded, "What was all that nonsense about aiming?"

"I have a feel for guns. I used to hunt rabbits when I was seven years old. You will need to aim your firearm, so take your time and try to hit the watermelon."

Mark took aim with the service revolver and then for some unknown reason, he closed his eyes. His shot missed. He not only missed the watermelon, he missed the biggest barn in the county. Steve looked wide-eyed at his friend. Not even in his wildest imagination did he think Mark could be that bad. "Alright Sam, first of all don't close both your eyes. You need to keep at least one eye open. Keep your mind firm, keep your hand firm, and keep your weapon firm. Shut everything else out of your mind but hitting the target."

There was little improvement over the next half an hour. Mark fired more than twenty shots and hit the barn seven times, but he never did hit the watermelon. Steve was now genuinely worried; it was impossible that Laird could be worse than his friend. Steve was thinking that Sam's only hope was for Laird not to show. However, less than half a mile away, on the other side of Gold Hill, a bucket was hanging from a nail at the entrance of a disused mine. Laird and his second had hung the bucket there for a target. (Each bullet that hit the bucket had produced a ringing echo from the shaft.) The bucket was full of holes; Laird had hit his target more times than he had missed, and when he did miss the bucket, it was never by much

Satisfied with his preparation, Laird and his second started to make for the base of Gold Hill; on their way they would have to pass Hampton's barn. As they approached the barn, they could hear a rapid firing of shots. In his frustration, Steve had hastily put several holes in the watermelon. Mark had not fired a shot in the last couple of minutes; he was mesmerized by Steve's sudden activity. Mark had stood there frozen, pointing his gun at the watermelon while his friend had virtually cut the melon in half.

Just as Laird was able to make out Twain's figure from a distance, Steve had also seen Laird out the corner of his eye. Gillis quickly moved to Mark's far side and shot off the head of a mud-hen that happened by the barn. It fluttered and fell to the ground right below the watermelon.

"Yes, nice shot, Sam. But if you're finished with the watermelon there's no need to shoot off the heads of defenseless birds!" Gillis raised his voice in order for Laird to hear. Laird could now see the headless mud-hen flapping in the dirt by the barn door.

Laird turned to his second, who stared open-mouthed and started shaking his head. Laird looked first at the headless bird, and then back toward his adversary. To take a mud-hen's head off in mid-flight was an unbelievable shot.

After a brief discussion with his second, Laird walked up to Twain and begged his indulgence. He told Twain that he had no wish to commit suicide, and that if it was all right he would quietly leave town and there would be no need to continue with this affair. Gillis was just about to speak, but Twain clamped a hand on his shoulder to silence him. Twain gave a conciliatory smile to his opponent and told Laird that he had no wish to kill him either. The two shook hands, and Laird and his second turned to leave.

After they were safely out of view, Mark sank to the ground. His heart had been racing the whole time and how he had managed to present a calm exterior to Laird was in it-self remarkable. However, he knew he owed everything to his friend, whose ability with a gun had been matched with some very fast thinking. Mark sat on the ground and looked up at his friend.

Steve smiled a broad smile "I told you I wouldn't let you die!"

 **4) Jung Lo, 1866**

The old Chinese woman had gone as far as the old stone bridge. She walked with difficulty, but she wanted to be with her son a little longer before she said goodbye. She felt it would be the last time they would ever see each other. The son was feeling the same pain of separation, but knew he could not stay in the village he had grown up in, because it would be the village he would die in, if he did not take this opportunity to go now. His father had died a few years earlier, a poor and a prematurely old man who had known nothing except a hard existence scraping a living from the land. Jung Lo did not want the same fate. He kissed his mother at the bridge and turned. He did not look back. He walked rapidly with his Chinese queue bouncing from side to side behind his head. From the bridge the old woman watched his disappearing figure, until she could see him no more.

Jung Lo was born just outside Hangzhuo, in China's Zhejian Province, in 1844. His family had been poor farmers for centuries and his only real prospects were to become a poor farmer too. As a sign of his poor background, Jung Lo wore the pigtail of serfdom. Slightly built and barely five feet tall, he was, however, very fit. He had a natural ability for gymnastics, and as a youngster often thought of joining an acrobatic team. But his teenage years had come and gone without realizing that dream. He had made the journey to Shanghai on several occasions, and while in the city he heard of the new land of America. Wonderful stories of great wealth and unlimited opportunities. After one of his visits to Shanghai, he told his mother he wanted to go across the sea to California. The year was 1866.

The Central Pacific was losing railroad workers to the silver mines of Virginia City at an alarming rate. Those that didn't leave for the mines were lost to days of drunken inactivity, which was markedly worse after the men were paid. Charles Crocker, one of the pioneers of the Central Pacific, was told the only reliable workers were the Chinese. They only drank tea and hardly ever fought among themselves. Building the railroad out from Sacramento, the Central Pacific needed to get as far east as possible before the Union Pacific, building the railroad out of Omaha, got too far west. First, though, the Central Pacific had to overcome the unfriendly Sierra Nevada Mountains. Several tunnels would have to be knocked through their impossibly hard granite.

It was Central Pacific's ambition to beat Union Pacific to the Utah/Wyoming border. Union Pacific was laying track west from Nebraska, but they too had their fair share of problems, not the least of which were hostile Indians. However, Central Pacific's progress through the Sierra was extremely slow. The tunneling was measured not in feet but in inches. Several accidents had happened with black powder, and the men wanted more money.........., money that the Central Pacific could not afford. In the need for speed nitro-glycerin replaced the black powder. But then accidents increased in number and severity. Many went on strike over conditions and more pay. The company agreed only to stop using the nitro-glycerin.

Despite the complaints of their white counterparts, the Chinese didn't voice their objections. So it became almost the exclusive job of the Chinese to hammer, drill, and set charges. They worked in teams of three: one man would hold a drill bit against the granite, a second would pound a six-inch hole into the rock, and a third filled the hole with powder. Several teams of three worked side by side, as an indentation twelve-feet wide and ten-feet high slowly took shape.

At the beginning of 1866, there were more than a thousand Chinese working on the Central Pacific. Despite their efforts, work was still progressing too slowly for the owners. Charles Crocker wanted more Chinese to join the railroad. News of this reached Shanghai in the spring, and many more Chinese boarded ships bound for San Francisco. One of those that heeded the call was Jung Lo. He spent several weeks at sea in cramped quarters with other Chinese men. Despite poor sanitation, seasickness, dysentery, and the odd case of Yellow Fever, the men never complained. The Chinese cared for their sick, cleaned their quarter's every day, and buried their dead at sea.

In San Francisco, the ships were met by Central Pacific representatives. Jung Lo and the other Chinese coming off the Pacific clipper were transferred to boats headed up the delta to Sacramento. From Sacramento they went by rail to Dutch Flat, and then by ox carts up to where the gangs were laying beds for the new railroad. Hundreds of tents were spread over the immediate area. As the Chinese arrived they were largely ignored by the white workers. They were met at camp by a half-dozen Chinese who had been working on the railroad for a while. They were given tea and told what their jobs would be. Half a dozen men would share one small tent, and their work would go around the clock and continue through all types of weather. Each man was given two blankets and shown to the tent they would share. They would observe the work in progress and were expected to imitate what they saw. They were told not to have anything to do with the mostly white track-layers and to ignore their insults. Their pride was to come from their work and how quickly it was finished. They were to be paid at the end of the month at three dollars a day, in gold coin.

Jung Lo watched and observed how his fellow Chinese worked. He saw a man holding a drill bit grimace when he was accidentally hit by a hammer, but through the obvious pain the man didn't cry out. He noticed more than a couple workers were missing fingers. He watched everyone retreat a safe distance when charges of black powder were primed and lighted. Following the explosions, he observed how quickly the men cleared the debris and repeated their tasks. Jung Lo was teamed up with two of his tent mates. It was mid-summer and they were told of the necessity for speed. With the influx of new Chinese workers, it was decided to work on tunnels from both directions. More than two hundred Chinese were transported by ox wagons over the summit to make a new working encampment above Donner Lake. Jung Lo and his two companions were part of this new eastside crew.

As the railroad proceeded eastward over the Sierra Nevada Mountains, telegraph poles were erected directly along-side the track. By the time the Chinese were transported to the new operations, the telegraph wire was already strung to the top of the trail. The wire had been temporarily rerouted, while the tunnels were being built, to a hut on the western side of the summit. The single hut was manned by two permanent telegraph operators that updated Sacramento on how work progressed. As yet, the wire did not go beyond Donner Summit; it wouldn't be extended down the eastern range of the Sierra until the track and tunnels were completed. One of the telegraph operators, Ralph McPherson, stood at the open door of the hut as the ox carts filled with Chinese workers, bound for the new operations, went by. Ralph waved as he recognized the big frame of the Irish foreman, who sat beside the driver of the lead cart.

Michael Sullivan was the bearded Irish foreman put in charge of this crew. Sullivan would oversee all aspects of the Chinese work. On his signal, fuses were lit, and when he blew his whistle everyone knew to take cover. Fuses were set alight by flint lighters, and even though Sullivan had only one hand he was capable of using a flint lighter quicker than any two-handed man. Sullivan had fought for the Union during the Civil War and had his left arm amputated after being wounded at the Battle of Fredericksburg. Like many ex-soldiers, he had drifted west after the war. Most of the rail workers working for the Union Pacific out of Omaha, Nebraska, were Civil War veterans. However, in California the Chinese became an ever-increasing presence. Sullivan did not socialize with the Chinese, but he had grudging respect for their work ethic and sobriety.

Jung Lo learned a few English words. He knew the meanings of "good" and "no good." All the Chinese learned the phrase "Fire in the hole." Still, Sullivan would always blow a whistle when charges were ready to be to be lit. Accidents became less frequent as the crews educated themselves and the teams worked in harmony. Jung Lo and his two compatriots soon became proficient at the work. His two tent partners took turns holding the drill bit and packing the powder, but because of his strength it was always Jung Lo who swung the hammer. The work was still arduously slow, but with teams now on opposite sides of the summit, overall progress was now twice as quick.

Summer faded into fall, and the days became cooler and the nights became cold. The skies became cloudier and the wind whistled around the mountain peaks. Vast amounts of logs were cut and split for the campfires. Fires were kept burning through-out, day and night. In November, the snows became more constant. More Chinese came, and separate crews were dedicated to shoveling snow.

By the end of 1866, the number of Chinese had grown to several thousand. Interested visitors from Sacramento and San Francisco would come to see the work, and their first sight was of smoke coming from more than a hundred camp-fires. There was the noise of a hundred hammers, followed by an eerie silence, followed by half a dozen heavily accented voices shouting, "Flien tha hal," Sullivan's whistle, a succession of explosions, and the sound of rocks being thrown out of the way. Through this the Chinese drank huge quantities of tea specially brought over from China and ate a steady diet of noodles and steamed vegetables. While one crew worked, another crew slept in their tents, ready to take over at the start of their shift. The routine continued around the clock. Sullivan worked most of the daylight hours and was relieved by another foreman working a twelve-hour shift. After dark the crews worked by torchlight.

In January, the snows became heavy and work was markedly slower. On snowy days there were more men clearing snow than there were making the tunnel. Between storms the sun would usually shine, and work progressed at a better rate. However, in the middle of January it snowed for six days straight. That was followed by a warmer spell and days of rain. The snow began disappearing on the lower mountain, but at the higher elevation it snowed more. Unknown to the Chinese and Mike Sullivan, there was unbearable pressure building from the excessive snow on top of the mountain and the supporting snow that was disappearing downhill.

Mike Sullivan initially thought the rain was a blessing, and was even more delighted when the sun eventually shone on a crisp late January day. Everything seemed to be progressing well, but then Sullivan heard a distant noise above the workings. Casually, he glanced upward and saw a ridge of snow give way. The initial noise was followed by several more, as more ridges gave way. The Chinese were largely unaware of the noises and the impending disaster that would kill most them. Sullivan started feverishly blowing his whistle, which caught the Chinese by surprise. Those who had stopped working saw Sullivan pointing up at the mountain, Sullivan was shouting "Avalanche!", but few Chinese knew the word. Some, however, could now see a huge volume of snow rushing down toward them. While others were transfixed, Jung Lo dived behind a large boulder.

He covered his face with his hands and kept his head down where the boulder curved at its base, giving him a pocket of air to breathe. The noise of the onrushing snow was deafening, like the roar of several freight trains. It was the loudest sound that Jung Lo had ever heard. There were sounds like pistol shots as trees snapped and broke. Jung Lo could not hear the muffled cries of his fellow countrymen being swept away. Dozens were tossed and dragged several hundred feet down toward the lake, and most of them were dead before the avalanche stopped. As the rivers of snow flowed all around him, Jung Lo feared his life would soon end.

He braced himself against the rock. The snow pushed with tremendous pressure as it filled nearly every conceivable crevice. Jung Lo had trouble keeping it out of his mouth, nostrils, and ears. He tried to form a barrier with his upper body to save a breathing space beneath his chin. Still, the snow pushed violently at his back and flowed through his legs with such force that it would have swept a smaller boulder off the mountain. Suddenly, the roar of the snow came to an end and the temperature dropped dramatically. The torrent of snow was over, and as it hardened, more oxygen filled the gaps. But now it was cold, dark, and silent. He was trapped beneath tons of snow. He had survived a quick death by drowning, only to face a slow death by hypothermia.

One of his knees was jammed beneath the rock, and his torso was wedged so tight that he had managed to stop the snow from filling a sixteen-square-inch gap below his chest. The rest of him was held motionless by a body armor of packed snow; it pressed against his spine and cradled the back of his head like a tight-fitting skull cap. Still, with the space he had managed to save, he was able to slide a little further beneath the rock. In the confined space he was just able to maneuver his arm. He slid his hand down to a small pack attached to his belt and extracted a spare drill bit. With his hand tight against his waist he started to scrape the tightly packed snow at his side. He worked the drill bit further up his body, trying to carve enough room to free both arms and to give him extra breathing space. He kept calm and labored inch by inch. After more than hour, he had managed a hole big enough to move his head. His legs were turned awkwardly and he couldn't move either of them.

In the darkness, he was uncomfortable but he was alive. He continued scraping, working a little lower so he could free the rest of his body. After a time he had enough freedom around his hips to shift his torso, but his legs were still trapped. Because his fingers were numbingly cold, the drill bit became increasingly difficult to hold, while the rest of his body was hot. He worked to free his knees, and then maybe he could reach down to his feet. It was a good while before he managed enough room around his knees to bend them slightly. He slid his upper body down enough so he could attack the snow around his feet. It could have been another hour before he was able to move his whole body. Exhausted, and struggling against the urge to sleep. He shook his hands and kicked his feet, to make warmer blood flow to his extremities. He continued on to create enough space so he could sit upright.

Had the crew on the other side of the summit known of the avalanche, they might have attempted a search for survivors. What they would have found would have been a totally different landscape than the one that has existed before. All evidence that there had been an encampment of two hundred men was gone. Half of those who were still breathing after the avalanche would die of their injuries. Bodies buried in the avalanche wouldn't be found again until early summer.

From being able to sit, he had gone to a kneeling position. He chipped away at the snow above his head. His progress was slow but eventually he was able to stand. The chipped snow fell, but didn't melt. He was going to tunnel his way straight up and chisel small steps as he went. He cut two small steps and climbed off the ground. A little further up and the bit hit something hard. It surprised him so much that he dropped the bit. His worst fear of losing his tool was now a real possibility. He dropped to the ground beneath him and blindly felt the area with his hands. It was a desperate ten minutes before he found it again.

He climbed back up the hole. He chipped a little more gingerly this time. It was solid. Jung Lo sensed it must be wood, which he guessed must be a tree that had been swept down with the force of the avalanche. Keeping a firm grip on the bit, he managed to work out where above his head the tree lay. He worked around it. Squeezing through the branches, he made further progress upwards until he hit another tree. Cautiously he worked around each tree, as well as a few boulders. On occasion, the chipped steps would not hold his weight and he would slip a few feet down. At times Jung Lo made use of the trees he passed to rest. It was tiring work, and despite being surrounded by snow he was hot as he struggled ever upward. At last he could see some evidence of light above him, he guessed that morning had turned to afternoon and he was not sure how much daylight might be left.

As Jung Lo broke through to the surface, a cold fresh wind hit his face. The sun was still above the mountains, but it would only last for another hour or so. His surroundings were unrecognizable. Nothing remained that was familiar to him. The odd broken tree stuck out from a vast expanse of snow. What was left of a torn tent had wrapped itself around a limb and flapped in the wind. Pieces of a broken powder barrel lay smashed as if it had been pushed off a hundred-foot cliff. The avalanche had destroyed everything in its path. Jung Lo was awestruck by the completeness of the destruction. Could he be the only one alive?

He estimated the avalanche must have happened more than five hours earlier, yet there was not a single human to be seen. Had the avalanche killed everyone? Were there others beneath the snow still alive? Should he look or go for help? Could he walk over the snow? How far could he get before night fell? The obvious direction was to walk downhill to the trail, which led back over the summit, but there was no chance he could get to the western camp before dark. He would try to get as far as he could, and maybe he could find some kind of shelter against the coming night and its subzero temperatures.

As he walked, slipped, and slid his way downhill, he thought he could see something ahead which was different from the debris of rocks and bits of tree on the snow's surface. He made his awkward way down toward it. As he came closer he could see it was a man's jacket. Although the jacket was moving in the wind, it was somehow fixed to the snow. As he got closer he could see the jacket was draped over something that held it in place. Jung Lo knelt and flipped the jacket over to reveal the head and a shoulder of a man protruding above the snow.

The man's eyes were closed and there was no visible sign that he was still alive. The head was tilted forward, and at first Jung Lo had no idea who it was. He gently moved the man's head back. Jung Lo recognized the frozen features of his foreman Mike Sullivan. Using his drill bit, Jung Lo feverishly dug a space around the Irishman's shoulders. He worked with inspired vigor to free the big man. After a short time he had enough space to put his arm under the Irishman's one good arm. With super human strength, the small framed Chinaman hauled the big Irishman out.

Jung Lo dragged the Irishman on his back by his ankles down the hill. He didn't know whether the foreman was alive or not, but he thought if he could at least start a fire there was more chance of reviving him. Having gotten down the hill, Jung Lo dragged the Irishman along to the edge of the path of destruction to where the trees still stood. There were fallen pine cones and pine needles in abundance, which he collected by the armload. He pried loose bark from every available tree. Here and there were fallen branches and other pieces of wood. Leaving the unconscious Irishman, Jung Lo ran back to the tent and the smashed barrel he had seen before. He unraveled the tent from the fallen tree. From among the broken parts of the barrel he found a handful of powder. He stuffed the powder in his pockets and carried the remnants of the barrel and tent in his arms.

Jung Lo searched through Sullivan's pockets and found his flint lighter, which he knew the foreman always carried. Jung Lo ripped the sleeve off Sullivan's jacket, the unused sleeve that Sullivan usually tucked in his trousers. Jung Lo tore at the fibers and pushed them under a pile of pine cones, sprinkled some of the powder on top of the fibers, and struck the flint. The powder flashed and the fibers burst into flame. The cones needed some coaxing, but they, too, caught fire. Jung Lo carefully added needles and stacked bark on top to create a chimney effect. Once all was ablaze, Jung Lo put the bigger pieces of wood on. The fire took on a life of its own and started to give off some real heat. Up to now Jung Lo had been robotically doing everything, but now he started to thaw physically and mentally. He started to cry and shake as the heat brought feeling back to his body.

He turned his attention to Sullivan. It was as if the big man was frozen solid. He moved the Irishman as close to the fire as possible, but even then he knew it would not be enough. The daylight was now failing fast, and in the murkiness of an ending day, Jung Lo scampered high and low for every conceivable piece of timber, wet or dry. He piled hundreds of cones and smaller branches on top of the tent and dragged them to the fire. He found the stump of an old tree trunk, which he managed to loosen and, with difficulty, push, roll and drag to the fire. He had the idea to build a second fire on the other side of Sullivan. He had no powder left, but, using a couple of burning branches from the original fire, he was able to set fire to another pile of pinecones. Shortly there were two fires burning twenty feet apart, giving warmth to both sides of the unconscious Irishman.

Half a mile away, Ralph McPherson put another log into the Franklin stove; he was alone in the hut on the summit. His colleague had to go down to Sacramento on compassionate leave, due to an ailing father. It was the last unused log inside the cabin. Once he had finished his coffee, he would have to grab an armful of new logs from the stack underneath the tarpaulin outside. As he stepped outside into the coolness of night, he stood and gazed skyward. He never lost his wonder for the mountain sky on a clear, moonless night; the stars were so numerous and so close he felt he could almost touch them. It was like looking at heaven. There was something overpowering and intimidating about the sight of a million stars. How could so much existence exist? He was almost paralyzed to the spot, momentarily forgetting his purpose in coming outside. His eyes followed the greatest band of stars which stretched directly over his head. As his eyes got to the eastern sky, he noticed an orange glow nearer to the horizon. It was not a natural light. McPherson ran through the snow to a higher vantage point, and the light became brighter and redder. Something was on fire!

Jung Lo felt he had done all he could do, and whether Sullivan survived or not was now out of his hands. He sat there transfixed by the flames. He sat on his haunches, and once his front became warm he turned around and gave his back some warmth. As he sat with his back to the fire he stared at a tree that stood by itself. The avalanche had probably run out of power by the time it reached this huge Douglas fir. Or maybe it had just refused to go down. It was a good sixty feet away from the rest of the forest. He looked up to see how close the branches spread to its nearest neighbor, and he knew it was a safe enough distance. The fir was close to a hundred feet high. It was bound to make a spectacular fire. If he could set it alight, just maybe someone somewhere would see it from afar.

Charles Crocker left Sacramento the day after word came down about the avalanche and a terrible loss of life on the eastern side of the summit. On seeing the devastation for himself, Crocker immediately announced that operations on the eastern side would be halted until late spring, when all the snow had melted and the dead had been recovered. Apparently, there had been a dozen Chinese survivors who were now being treated for their injuries. Only one person had walked away with no injury at all. Crocker met the small, plucky Jung Lo, and through an interpreter learned that he had set a Douglas fir ablaze. The blaze had been seen by the telegraph operator on top of Donner Summit. A handful of survivors had also made their way to the blazing tree and joined Jung Lo.

Crocker thanked Jung Lo for his efforts and was just about to leave when one of the foremen from the western side of the summit came to Crocker. The foreman told Crocker that Jung Lo had been responsible for rescuing an unconscious Mike Sullivan from certain death. Crocker turned to Jung Lo again and thanked him more enthusiastically. He told the interpreter that Jung Lo's act of compassion would be well remembered. Jung Lo asked through the interpreter after Mister Sullivan's health. Crocker assured him that, as soon as he knew, he would make it a point that Jung Lo was told.

Charles Crocker took his leave of the young hero but continued in conversation with the foreman.

Sullivan awoke in bed to an unfamiliar room and fought to collect his thoughts. He was bandaged, his body ached, and his head throbbed. He saw a nurse come into the room. As she bent over to look into his eyes, her voice was soft and reassuring. "Well, Mr. Sullivan, you are a marvel. You have been unconscious for more than a week! You owe your life to a small Chinaman who dragged you off the mountain. I think he will be very happy to hear you are still with us. More than two hundred others were not so lucky."

It was three weeks later when Sullivan returned to Donner Summit. He had not seen Jung Lo while in hospital. He had wanted to thank him personally for saving his life. Upon arrival at the western camp, he went to visit some of the Chinese, but no one knew where Jung Lo was. After an afternoon of fruitless search, it was obvious to Sullivan that Jung Lo had gone. Eventually, Sullivan spoke to the foreman who had spoken to Charles Crocker four weeks earlier.

Only Mr. Crocker and the foreman had known the intentions of the young Chinaman.

Jung Lo walked along the trail underneath the tall bamboo which creaked in the wind. He had been given three months off with pay until the operations were to restart in the late spring. He walked the trail between the rice fields on either side, and only stopped when he came to the old stone bridge of his village.

 **(5) The Hole in Lake Tahoe, 1869**

October 1869

Silver mining operations at the Savage Mine in Virginia City had been halted for a period of six months over the previous winter, due to uncontrollable underground flooding. The water pumps, brought over from England, had been ineffective during that time. Then suddenly last April they had rendered even the lowest shaft dry. Through May and June mining had been very productive. Then in early July the shafts flooded once more and operations were brought to a halt. By the end of July renewed pumping made the water recede a second time. August and September saw another rewarding period of mining. But now in October the shafts were flooded again.

Like many, Jack Jameson, one of the Savage Mine foremen, was puzzled. Why should the pumps be so successful at one time and so utterly useless at other times? As Jameson was lost in his thoughts, his pit boss called him.

"What do you make of that, Jameson?"

"Damned if I know, boss, there's got to be a logical explanation. Seismic shift of some sort? Maybe we need to call in a geologist."

"What are you talking about? I mean that. What do you make of THAT?" The boss was pointing down to a bulky object which floated aimlessly around the flooded lower level.

Jameson strained his eyes by the light of the lamp to see, refusing to believe them. The bulky object was a body.

"Whatever, or whoever it is, get it out of there Jameson."

With the help of four men, Jameson managed to lift the body from its watery grave. The back of the victim's head was badly gashed, though the water had washed the wound clean of any blood. It was a middle-aged man, the gash perhaps due to hitting his head after a fall. However, the main question on Jameson's mind was, who was he?" Nobody seemed to know. He was not an employee. The guards checked everyone in and out of the mine. They had no clue to the man's identity. The dead man was well dressed and obviously no miner. So where had he come from?

April 1869

William Meeker trimmed his cigar. He was delighted with Tahoe's serenity and inspired by her size and beauty. It was a bright, sunny, spring morning. The sky was a glorious blue and the lake was as flat as a mill pond. While smoking his cigar, seated on the cabin's porch, he decided to take the dinghy out for an hour or so before breakfast.

Carnelian Bay, on Lake Tahoe's northwest shore, was the site of a small lumber camp and half a dozen log cabins, one of which Meeker had rented for six months. He pulled the wooden dinghy over the pebbled beach and launched it into the clear water. He clambered on board, sat his stout frame down between the two oars, and started to row. His oars made lazy circles in the lake's calm surface, and the rowing was virtually effortless. As he filled his lungs with a couple of deep breaths of Tahoe air, the dinghy glided easily on. All that was audible was the sound of the oars going in and out of the water.

He was some two hundred yards off shore. All seemed peaceful, until he discovered that despite his gentle and even rowing stroke, the dinghy was not going straight. He stopped, the dinghy started circling. As he observed in amazement, the circles became ever smaller. William Meeker realized that he must be floating over some kind of whirlpool. Amused at first, he then gave it a little more thought. Was there a hole draining water out of Lake Tahoe? He rowed the dinghy off the whirlpool, so he could see from a better vantage point. Through calmer waters he could vaguely see, maybe fifty feet beneath the water's surface, the whirlpool tightening as it drained through a hole in the lake's bottom. Meeker looked at his surroundings and made note of his proximity from shore, the point beyond the bay, and where it was in relation to the cabin. He fixed all of this to his memory, so if he needed to relocate the exact position, he would feel fairly confident in finding the whirlpool again.

He rowed back to the cabin. Too excited to have breakfast, he thought more and more on his discovery. He was fixated by one thought, and he could only imagine where this thought might lead him. Meeker decided to cable his friend Colonel Clare, a stockbroker in San Francisco: "COME TO CARNELIAN BAY TAHOE URGENT W.M." Colonel Clare arrived forty-eight hours later. They had known each other for some time and had mutual respect for each other's integrity. So when Colonel Clare received William's strange cable, he did not question it. Upon hearing about William's experience on the lake, and the deduction he had come to, Colonel Clare was more than a little intrigued. It was too late to take the dinghy out that evening, but they agreed to rediscover the hole at first light.

"Well, what do you think?" William asked as Colonel Clare looked over the side of the dinghy. It was another beautiful morning and the two had wasted no time getting out on the lake.

"Between two and three foot in diameter, I would say." Colonel Clare had a big smile on his face. "I think you might have just found the cause of the problem and given us a chance at a substantial fortune!" The problem Colonel Clare referred to was the unexplained flooding of the silver mines in Virginia City, and in particular the flooding of the Savage Mine, which was the deepest mine of the Comstock Lode. "If we can plug it, maybe we can control events to our advantage. We need a conical plug maybe two feet high, three and a half feet wide at the top, narrowed down to two foot wide at the bottom."

The two friends approached the local lumber camp. Finding a pine tree suitable was not difficult, but cutting and shaping a conical plug took the skills of an experienced lumberjack. It was a strange request but the camp manager asked no questions. Once shaped, the plug was secured to a sixty-foot chain by means of a railroad spike. To the other end of the chain they attached a steamer buoy. William and the colonel were anxious to try the plug out as soon as everything was completed. The plug and chain weighed more than a hundred and fifty pounds and it took their combined efforts to gently load it on board the dinghy.

They rowed to the whirlpool and dropped the plug over the side. The plug and chain descended quickly and were caught by the vortex and sucked into position. With a jolt the buoy was pulled under the surface, but with a gush it reappeared seconds later. It had worked. The whirlpool was gone, the buoy was floating on a placid lake, and the two friends rejoiced. Their moment of victory was short lived. Because the plug was stuck fast, neither man could free it. They pulled together, as hard as they could without capsizing the dinghy. They pulled and pulled but the plug would not move.

Undeterred, they left the buoy afloat and returned ashore. Again at the lumber camp, they paid to have a winch fitted. Winches were used at the lumber camps to haul cut logs aboard the ox wagons. The winch was purposely blocked into the stern of the dinghy so it could withstand more than five hundred pounds of stress. Rowing back to the buoy, while the colonel kept the dinghy steady, William attached the chain to the winch. Meeker positioned his weight for balance as the hand-cranked winch took the strain. Using both hands, he pulled at the handle. After a moment of obstinacy, the plug freed, the whirlpool came back into life and the boat started circling. They tested plugging and unplugging two more times before they finally hoisted the buoy. With the chain and plug on board, they rowed back to the cabin. That night

Colonel Clare returned to San Francisco, leaving William to safeguard their interests at the lake.

The San Francisco stock market was small and all the brokers knew each other. No one before doubted Colonel Clare's judgment; he was known for his caution and good sense. So why was he now buying up the stock in the Savage Mine?

"The Savage Mine is worthless," said one broker to another.

"Then why is Clare buying at every turn?" asked the other.

"I don't know, but look at the facts: half the shafts are flooded, the water continues to rise, and the pumps are useless to prevent it. The Savage Mine is past tense! Clare is either suffering from a mental breakdown or needing a business write-off. I advise you to sell!"

Colonel Clare had never enjoyed himself more. He had spent a busy day buying up the seemingly obsolete Savage Mine. Many times he was asked why he was buying, but he would just state that he was willing to buy any stock at a very fair price. By the end of three days of buying, Colonel Clare was the Savage Mine's majority stockholder.

William Meeker trimmed a cigar. His reaction upon hearing Colonel Clare's news was one of elation. "Brilliant!" Then a cloud of doubt passed over his face. "What if they don't pump the mine, thinking it useless to attempt it?"

"Not a problem. As majority stockholder, I shall insist they do!"

"Brilliant!" Meeker spluttered through his cigar, excited again.

"Let's get the plug in place first thing tomorrow. I can't be away too long." By the following afternoon, Colonel Clare was on the train back to San Francisco. The two conspirators had successfully plugged the hole earlier that morning.

At the Savage Mine in Virginia City the following day, the pit boss went to see Jameson. "We've had a cable from that new owner fella. He wants us to try the pumps again. I guess we had better do as he says, but these owners haven't got a clue what we're up against here."

Two days later, the pit boss was astounded to hear Jameson report that the waters were down more than fifty feet.

"We'll see how tomorrow's pumping goes first before we tell this new owner."

The pumps were started earlier the next day. At the end of the day, Jameson reported to his boss. "The water's down nearly a hundred feet, all told. Another five days like this and we'll be able to start mining again!"

A week of pumping, and all the shafts were dry. Not daring to believe it, the pit boss cautiously gave the go-ahead for operations to restart.

New men were hired, and silver veins that had been submerged beneath water for months were reworked. Slowly and steadily the amount and quality of ore improved. By the end of May, the Savage Mine was producing as much silver as any other mine on the Comstock.

It was a truly remarkable turn-around.

July 1869

William Meeker, still in Carnelian Bay, had done his level best to keep up with the Savage Mine reports. He had begun to wonder if just being an owner of a successful mine was not reward enough. He was like a proud father as he saw the mine produce more and more good quality ore. Just as Meeker was feeling flushed with pride a cable came from San Francisco: "HAVE STARTED TO SELL STOCK WILL RETURN NEXT WEEK CLARE."

On his return to Carnelian Bay, Colonel Clare explained that he had sold all the stock, and had deposited in excess of a million dollars in profit into a new bank account. Delighted with the news, Meeker did, however, mention his earlier thought that it had been nice to see the mine do so well and be a part of its success.

"No!" had been Clare's emphatic response. Clare illustrated his argument in telling his friend that it was they that controlled fate and not fate that controlled them. If they stayed with the mine, they would have to run the gauntlet of possible cave-ins, explosions, poisonous gases, or even the discovery of no new silver. To get in quick, turn a handsome profit, and get out quick was the best policy.

Meeker bowed to Clare's better understanding. "Yes, I guess you're right. A million dollars is a handsome profit."

The colonel clapped his hand on Meeker's shoulder. "Yes, my friend, this was a once-in-a-lifetime opportunity!" Clare winked. "And we'd be foolish not to do it again!"

Meeker started to choke on his cigar "What!!!?" he blurted.

"Come on, think about it. We did it once, we can do it again! A million dollars is good. A million apiece is even better!"

"It's preposterous! We'll be found out!"

"It's not as preposterous as your face, and I will do it with or without you!"

Meeker wanted out but it was too late. The colonel had all the cards. He controlled everything: the events, the money, and him. He was beginning to wish he had not let Colonel Clare in on his discovery. The next morning, the two men pulled the plug again.

Everyone at the Savage Mine was frustrated. The pumps were not working as they had back in April, and the flooding was again uncontrollable. There was much consternation at the San Francisco stock exchange too. Shareholders watched the value of the Savage Mine shares slide more and more. A group of brokers on the floor of the exchange came up to Colonel Clare and commended him on his luck in getting out of the mine at just the right time. He tried to reassure them.

"My dear fellows the flooding is a temporary nuisance. I'm sure in a week or two there will be productive mining again. Just be patient."

"It's all right for you!" retorted a frustrated broker. "We've lost our shirts!"

"Again, I believe the flooding is temporary, and if you don't agree, I'll buy your stock at a third of your original purchase price. But don't come crying to me when the stock is up again!"

Despite Colonel Clare's words of encouragement, the Savage mining operations had to be abandoned. The stock was now worth barely ten cents on the dollar. Clare was inundated by brokers who wanted to sell. To those he had spoken to before, he did buy at a third of their original purchase price. To others he was not so generous. He was no fool and felt that by being too sensitive to everyone's bad luck might appear suspicious.

Over a further period of two weeks, Colonel Clare slowly became the Savage Mine's majority stockholder again.

Not long after that, the plug was back in the hole, the shafts were pumped dry, and the Savage Mine was back in business.

August and September were again productive and the stock price rose every week.

October 1869

It was early October when Colonel Clare was approached by one of the most eminent stockbrokers in San Francisco, Herbert Thorn. After a cordial greeting and some suitable small talk, Thorn mentioned he had been instructed by clients to make a reasonable offer for Clare's interest in the Savage Mine.

"A reasonable offer, you say. Would you like to enlighten me?" Clare casually inquired.

"I can see I will have to give you their best offer, and I am instructed to go as high as one million dollars." Thorn's superior indifference annoyed the colonel.

"You increase that offer by another half million and you have yourself a deal," countered Clare.

Thorn was a little less indifferent. "Colonel Clare, I happen to know you could not have spent more than three hundred thousand for your shares. With the mine susceptible to flooding, I suggest a million is a very generous offer!" Although still condescending, Thorn's voice was now clearly agitated.

"The flooding comes and goes, I'll agree. But when it goes, the ore being mined is of an exceptional quality! One and a half million and the stock is yours. A good day to you, sir," retaliated the colonel.

Two days later, Clare sold the stock to Thorn for one and a half million dollars. Having banked the money with the previous profit, the Colonel sent a cable to Carnelian Bay: "HAVE ACHIEVED GOAL C.C."

It had been a beautiful early autumn day at Carnelian Bay. The sun was still warm and the few aspen trees around the lake stood golden among the green pines. Another month and the first snows would come, and William Meeker would have to leave. It had been an enjoyable and peaceful six months, and now he was richer than he had ever dreamed. As he relaxed in an armchair, the late afternoon sun cast long shadows through the cabin windows. He clipped and lit a cigar and reflected on his good fortune.

His sublime solitude was interrupted by a sudden knock on the cabin door. It was the colonel. Clare explained his unexpected arrival by telling William he wanted to pull the plug for the last time. He had no liking for Thorn and it would give him great personal satisfaction to see Thorn's reputation ruined. Meeker suggested dinner, followed by a game of cards in front of the log fire, with brandy to toast their new found wealth. To William's surprise, Colonel Clare dismissed the suggestion and stated he wanted pull the plug that very evening.

The sun had disappeared behind the mountains by the time the two men started to row out on the lake. With daylight fading, it took a little longer to find the buoy. William Meeker hauled the buoy on board and attached the chain to the winch. Having successfully freed the plug, William continued to winch as Colonel Clare sat at the oars. Just as William got the plug to the surface, Clare remarked. "What a beautiful moonrise we have this evening, William."

William, who was facing the colonel, had to turn around to look at the moon. With Meeker's back toward him, Colonel Clare snatched the winch handle. With little noise he raised it high and swiftly brought it down hard on William's turned head. Meeker's body fell forward and lay motionless. Clare grabbed an arm and a leg and heaved the dead weight into the water.

Jameson came in to see his pit boss. "There is nothing to identify the man. He is well dressed. He has an expensive fob watch, a silk handkerchief, and one gold cigar trimmer."

 *(6) Three-Toed Island, 1870*

If ever there was a majestic setting worthy of the adjective, it had to be Eagle Bay. Eagle Bay was a virtual lake of its own, encircled by steep cliffs, except for a narrow opening into Lake Tahoe's southwest corner. Rising out of the bay's emerald green waters stood Lake Tahoe's only island.

The bay was the domain of the bald eagle, which kept an ever-watchful eye from its craggy throne high on the surrounding cliffs. In years before, the eagle had seen the occasional canoe enter the bay paddled by two Indians. More recently the eagle had watched the building of two log cabins, and the visitors who had come and gone. However, not until now had any human chosen to live permanently at the bay.

The first man to live through the harsh winters of Tahoe's southwest shore was late of Her Majesty's Navy. An English seafarer who had experienced the worst of Cape Horn was not one to fear any tantrum Tahoe could throw, even in her foulest mood. He had lived at Eagle Bay for the past eighteen months in splendid isolation. Once a week he would sail his fourteen-foot sloop the six miles over to the south shore community and buy his weekly provisions. Every week was a carbon copy of the week before. He would tie up at the south shore pier around noon. After eating lunch, he shopped at the general store where he bought his vittles and pipe tobacco. The last purchase was always his most precious:

a demi-john of whiskey, to tide him over for the six days he spent alone.

Having stowed his purchases aboard his boat, he would return to town to spend the rest of the evening drinking among friends at Rowland's Lake House. With his cheery disposition and pipe in mouth, the captain was always a welcome, once-weekly addition to the regulars of the smoke-filled saloon. For a few hours, the captain would socialize and down several shots of whiskey before leaving. Then, close to midnight, he would stagger back down to the pier, inebriated and sail back to Eagle Bay.

It was a fine early December morning when the captain left Eagle Bay to sail over to south shore. The day had been uneventful and the captain had received his usual warm greeting at Rowland's. He walked to a vacant stall at the bar, acknowledged all his friends, talked, listened, drank, and smoked for a good part of four hours. Then a newly arrived patron spoke.

"Best you stay here tonight, Cap'n. It's snowing outside."

"Yes, there's a definite storm in the offing," added another.

"No, lads, I'll sleep in my own bed. A little bit of snow aren't going to persuade me otherwise!"

The captain wished everyone a good night and staggered into the cold night air. The wooden pier was now covered in several inches of snow, and he gingerly stepped, fearing to slip. The wind was strong and the snow fell steadily as he tottered aboard his little boat. With haphazard hand strokes he cleared the snow off the boat's lines and untied her. He also cleared a space on the wooden seat and set sail.

The captain was just two miles offshore when the snow fell so hard that visibility could only be measured in feet. The wind was so erratic that it seemed to blow from every direction, and it tossed the little boat up and down and from side to side.

He was unable to keep his seat as waves battered the boat from all sides. He thought of running down the sail, but before he could do that simple task, a stronger gust of wind snapped the mast, and as it fell it knocked the Captain over-board. The coldness of the water had one advantage: he regained all the awareness of sobriety. Survival expectancy was a matter of minutes. Treading water, coughing, and spitting the captain strained every nerve to catch sight of his sloop. Every wave washed the breath from him. Every second, the aching cold became more intense.

A year and a half earlier, on a chance meeting in San Francisco, Captain Dick Barter had been introduced to Ben Holladay. Holladay, the famed stagecoach pioneer, had taken an immediate liking to the old English seafarer. Holladay liked the captain's honest expression, the grey eyes vivid in a weathered face of scars and wrinkles. The two had struck up an instant friendship on a mutual respect for each other's differing lifestyles. Captain Dick had accepted Ben Holladay's offer to accompany him on one of his stages up to Virginia City. En route, Holladay had suggested visiting his cabins on Eagle Bay at Lake Tahoe. They had taken a fourteen-foot sloop named *The Nancy* from south shore on a perfect June day. The captain had marveled at the beauty of the lake and the wonderful seclusion of the bay.

"Yes, it is beautiful," Holladay had commented. "But unfortunately the cabins fall into disrepair without proper care and attention. I need a permanent caretaker, but no man in his right mind would stay here all year round."

"I would!" the captain had cheerfully declared.

Ben Holladay, buoyed by his new friend's enthusiasm, described the harshness of a Sierra winter and the possibility of an enforced and undesired isolation. The captain had explained, in return, that in his many years at sea he was no stranger to the bitterness of winter weather.

In eighteen months the captain had never regretted coming to Lake Tahoe. But this night, he felt sure, would be his last. He repented his folly to the Almighty and asked for forgiveness for his many sins. The answering hand of God came on a crest of a wave, as the mast crashed upon the captain from behind. No longer in the last throes of life, the captain grabbed the mast with renewed vigor. Though the mast had snapped in two, it was still attached to the boat by its rigging. Hand over hand he pulled rigging and the boat toward him. The boat fought like an unbroken stallion, but the captain was like a man possessed. He pulled it closer and closer. Finally within an arm's-length, he grabbed the gunwale and with the strength of Poseidon hoisted himself back on board.

In the bottom of the boat there was now close to six inches of shipped water. The captain found his demi-john still corked, lying on its side. He wrenched the cork free and downed several life-giving swallows of fiery liquid, which spread throughout his body. He then stuck his numbed fingers into his mouth and sucked at each one to revive some sensitivity. He again drank deeply from the demi-john. His boat had been tossed every which way, he had no idea which direction was home, and there was no hope of getting back on course now. The broken mast dragged like an anchor in the lake. The storm had yet to subside and the boat bounced on each wave, but the Captain was beyond caring. He had no strength left. Totally spent, he re-corked the demi-john, and collapsed into a deep sleep.

The gray light of morning found the storm much less severe. A light snow still fell, but the wind was now just a gentle breeze. The clouds were higher and visibility grew as the last lingering mist vanished off the surface of the gray water. Some of the clouds still hung to the mountains, but everything at lake level was now clear. The storm had pushed the small boat an equal distance from either shoreline. The captain's face, as he slept, was facing up, but most of his head was submerged in the water inside the boat. He awoke and cautiously lifted his neck to find most of his body was also beneath water. Cold and wet through, he painfully lifted his head above the boat to see where he was. He was maybe three miles away from the bay and his cabin. The broken mast continued to bounce into the boat's side. The captain reached for his knife and, with difficulty, cut the rigging free. He watched the mast float away.

The top of Mount Tallac was obscured among the clouds, but its unmistakable shape was evident beneath. Renewing his vigor from his blessed demi-john, he untied the oars that were lashed under the seats. There were parts of his body that ached and other parts which he could not feel at all. Mechanically, he sat with the oars on either side and started to row. Even though the boat was only now and again lifted by a rogue wave, the progress was very slow. His neck was stiff, his clothes hung icy cold against his skin, and he was just about as uncomfortable as he had ever been. Sometimes the oars fell from his grasp and he would have to clap his hands together to get the blood circulating. He constantly stopped to take sustenance from the demi-john. After every swallow he shivered. After a painful two hours he reached the bay, he had rowed a distance which normally would have taken him barely thirty minutes.

Reaching the beach outside his cabin, he limped ashore. He left most of his new purchases in the boat, but he brought the demi-john and tobacco inside. To get dry and warm was his first concern. The cabin's walls were lined with cut firewood, and within minutes Captain Dick had a blazing fire going. It took all the effort he could muster to strip down to his long johns. He hung his heavy wet clothes to one side. Having stood before the fire long enough, he filled his pipe with damp tobacco and filled a glass with whiskey. He moved his favorite chair a comfortable distance from the flames and melted into it with his pipe and glass in hand. He toasted renewed life and sat there until hunger moved him to fix something to eat.

After he had taken breakfast the following morning, the captain was better able to take stock. He knew he needed help to repair his boat and started to plan for an early return to south shore. He had suffered little physical harm, but he noticed that three toes on his right foot had not recovered their healthy color and were in fact becoming blacker. The captain had seen gangrene before at sea, and he knew that this was his possible fate now.

Immediate attention to his toes meant forgoing any other plans he had intended. The blackened toes had obviously resulted from frost bite, and to stop the gangrene from spreading, the toes would have to come off. Amputations at sea were commonplace, and, without a good ship surgeon, many seamen died at the hands of incompetence. Following amputation, nerve endings of cut limbs would go into shock. Pain was temporarily retarded and bleeding was minimal. While pain and bleeding were slowed, a surgeon would have to work quickly. The captain was no coward, but this would take more than courage. A fine balance between keeping alert and numbing the pain would be needed. Just the right amount of Dutch courage; combined with a steady hand.

With the exception of the poker, which rested in the fire, the instruments the captain needed were laid out on the hearth: a knife, a chisel, a hammer, one brick, a towel, stripped pieces of bed linen, a bowl of water (melted snow,) a tall glass filled with whiskey, his demi-john and one sock. He proposed to down the whole glass before starting and, in the period before it took effect, get as much as he could stomach done. The captain had cut two holes in a sock, so the surviving big and little toe could protrude through. For want of company, he put his looking glass on the mantle. In many months of isolation the captain was in the habit of talking to himself. On the towel was a four-inch biting stick; after swallowing the glass of whiskey he would bite down on the stick and get to work.

It might have looked very ghoulish, but he had thought it through; it was important to take the toes off as quickly as possible. A hammer and chisel to get through the bone; place the chisel at the base of each gangrenous toe; a gulp of whiskey and - no hesitation - a swift decisive blow with the hammer. Maybe two gulps of whiskey, maybe three. He had everything he needed, it was all right there. There was nothing left to do but do it.

Actually, another talking-to was needed. He got the looking glass and talked to his reflection. "Only sensible thing to do," he told himself. "Lose three toes now or maybe a whole leg next week. Not possible to take your whole leg off by yourself. It's got to be done!" He reseated himself, and looked at his toes; it was gangrene, no doubt. He got up again and paced. He talked to himself again, "The sooner done, the sooner over!" There really was no alternative. He sat down again. He drank some whiskey, and he felt better, so he drank some more.

He was going to do it. He drank a bit more, got up, and adjusted the poker so it was in the hottest part of the fire. He could feel the whiskey taking effect. He sat down again. It was now or never.

He placed the stick between his teeth, pulled the towel over the brick, and planted his foot on top. He leaned forward, put the chisel at the base of his first gangrenous toe, raised the hammer above his head, and brought it down with as much force as he could muster. The flesh split, the bone cracked, and the bloody first toe was off. Tears welled up in his eyes as his teeth bit ever harder into the stick, but he had to keep going. Speed was of the essence now. He placed the chisel at the base of the second toe and again brought the hammer down with as much strength as he had. He placed the chisel at the base of third toe and fooled himself into thinking that the intense pain was due to the gangrene, and not because he had just butchered himself.

Two of the toes were completely off. The third toe was still attached by a piece of obstinate flesh. He stood up on his one good foot and reached for the poker. He immediately placed the hot tip of the poker to the gap between his remaining big toe and the toe which was tenuously still attached. There was a putrid smell of burning flesh accompanied by a searing pain, which sent a sudden rush of nausea to his nostrils. Still, his grim determination overcame his urge to pass-out and he put the poker to the bit of flesh that had kept the third toe from fully separating. The hot poker had lost some of its intensity and was not hot enough to free the toe from the foot. He took the stick out of his teeth, returned the poker to the fire, picked up the demi-john and swallowed directly from the bottle. Whiskey spilled from the corners of his mouth and ran down his chin.

He put the demi-john aside and sat down again. He picked up his pipe from the nearby table, filled it with tobacco, and lit it with the dried bark of an aspen, which he kept especially for the purpose. After some long draws on his pipe, the cabin filled with exhaled smoke. He carefully placed his butchered foot with its dangling toe into the bowl of water. The cold water increased the throbbing sensation, and he could only imagine how bad the pain might have been had he not had the whiskey inside him. He clamped his free hand to his head. He would not be defeated now, but he would have to wait for the poker to heat up again before he could finish. It was amateurish surgery, but it could have been a lot worse. The throbbing told him there could be hours if not days of continued pain, and he might have to ration his intake of whiskey for when the pain was at its most unbearable.

He felt physically drained, which was a good sign. Sleep would be a good healer and a deep sleep would alleviate pain for a while. He would give into the exhaustion once he was finished. But first he had to cauterize the foot completely and bind the wound. He would have to dress the wound on a daily basis. And there was probably not enough fresh bed linen, so he would need to boil what linen he had and reuse it.

The bowl of water was now a cloudy red, with little bits of flesh floating around his immersed ankle. He gingerly took the foot out. The toe still dangled, and as gently as he could he placed the foot on the already soiled towel. With the pipe in his mouth, he again carefully stood on his good foot and grabbed the poker. He put the glowing tip of the poker to burn off the obstinate flesh that kept the toe attached. The moist flesh sent a mixture of steam and smoke thick enough to obscure the captain from seeing clearly. He did not care about the pain; he just wanted it finished. So he pressed down with enough strength to burn a hole through the towel. He felt his foot slide a little and he knew his third and last toe had finally been detached.

A week later, the foot had been healing well and there was no sign of further infection. He had given the foot another round of cauterization, just to be sure. With the foot bound, he wore the modified sock, and he hobbled around as best he could. He would purposely give time each day to strip the bandages off and air the wound. He had been forced to miss his once-weekly visit to south shore and, despite rationing, he was out of whiskey. He had tobacco to last a few more days, but he felt unsure whether the foot would be healed enough to attempt his usual weekly trip even after another week. But no whiskey, a longer period of isolation, and three missing toes were a small price to pay for having saved his leg.

The weather had turned mild and the captain was seated on the step outside the cabin, resting his foot. In the sky, an osprey fish hawk circled above the bay, waiting to strike feet first on an unsuspecting trout. Just as the fish was unaware of the osprey, the osprey was unaware of the old seafarer. However, unknown to all three, a pair of sharper eyes were looking on. With huge dark wings and frightening quickness, the keen-eyed observer came swooping down from the surrounding cliffs. Skimming the water, its outstretched talons snatched at the surface. The attack and capture took a matter of seconds, and, despite a defiant struggle, the wriggling trout was lifted high and carried up to the cliffs. Robbed of its dinner, the startled osprey flew off, shrieking its futile objections to the bald eagle's act of piracy. The captain smiled to see the eagle would not suffer an intruder to its territory. He felt honored that eagle did not seem to mind to share the bay with him. From its high vantage point, the eagle initially ignored the writhing fish beneath its foot, and instead watched a boat pulling into the bay.

The boat had been in the bay ten minutes before the captain noticed it. The old seafarer's smile broadened to a grin as he recognized the half- dozen men on board. The south-shore locals had been concerned for the captain's well-being and when he had not arrived on his weekly visit they decided to see if he was all right!

"Ahoy there, my hearties!" shouted the captain.

"Well, here he is, boys, as right as a fiddle!" said the first local, as the men walked up to his cabin. "Caused us a lot of worry you did, Cap'n, not showing up like that," continued the local.

"Thought you'd be out of whiskey and tobacco, so we brought some," added a second.

The captain's face beamed. "Well you better come in," he said as he struggled to stand up.

The men crowded into the small cabin. Sharing the whiskey, they sat on the floor around the fire. The old seafarer, seated in his chair, told them of his experience.

"Cut your toes off? That's a bit hard to swallow, Cap'n," stated the first local.

The captain pointed to a glass on the mantle. "Care to have a drink from my last glass of whiskey? That you may find even harder to swallow!" he chuckled.

The local got up to look inside the glass. As he picked it up, he could see two or three objects in the darkened liquid. His face winced and his muffled cry got the other five friends to their feet. The captain burst out laughing as each one of his visitors' expressions changed as they recognized the contents of the glass.

"I had to keep my last drop of whiskey for me toes. I thought they would miss my foot less, if they had something to drink. They're a part of me. I couldn't just throw them away!"

"© **Collin Bogle.** Used with permission by MHS Licensing."

"With huge dark wings and frightening quickness,
the keen-eyed observer came sweeping
down from the surrounding cliffs."

Pony Express © Frank McCarthy, licensed by Greenwich Workshop, Inc.

Fannette Island – (Three-Toed Island)
© Sandy Pavel

**Outlet of Lake Tahoe before the turn
of the twentieth century**
Painting especially commissioned for this book
By local artist Keith Brown
© Keith Brown

The powdermonkeys-Cape Horn-1865 Autry National Center, Los Angeles; 2002.3.1 © Mian Situ

Lake Tahoe Bierstadt, Albert (1830-1902) Private Collection/Photo ©
Christie's Images/Bridgeman Art Library.
Possibly the first painting of Lake Tahoe 1860s

Fish Supper © Jean Louis Klein & Marie Luce Hubert

"He had known when the fish were
plentiful in the shallows of Lake Tahoe."
(The End of an Era)

Albert Bierstadt View from Donner Summit 1872
Central Pacific Railroad visible to the right, the rough
location of the *Jung Lo* story.
Part of the Donner party was stranded on the far shore of
the lake in 1846 -1847.

(7) The Dreaded Evening Drink (The Silent Terror), 1872

The big hands worked quickly. The axe arched high and crashed into the tall Jeffrey pine. The blade was stuck, but the big hands yanked it free and swung it again.

Big Jim Stewart stood six feet five inches tall and was one of the best lumberjacks around the camps of Tahoe. No one knew where he was originally from. Some said he was from Tennessee and he had fought for the South during the Civil War. Others said he was from Pennsylvania and he had fought for the North. Like many ex-soldiers, he had come out west to work on the Transcontinental Railroad during the mid and late 1860s. Some said they knew him when he worked in Nebraska for the Union Pacific. Others said he had been a tracklayer for the Central Pacific in Nevada. But no one ever asked Jim Stewart for the truth, because they knew Stewart would not take kindly to any questions.

The men would often talk about Jim Stewart, but they would never talk to him. His mean demeanor was notorious throughout the Tahoe area. He was paid extra, not just for his good work, but also to ensure the peace within the camp during working hours. The other men knew Stewart would not cause trouble while cutting timber, but he became the most feared man at the end of the day. Those big hands could free a gun from a holster quicker than an axe from a tree. And nobody came near Stewart when he drank.

There was at first a hesitant whine, followed by a more continual moan. As one big hand gave a helpful shove the moan turned into an ear splitting crack. The fated Jeffrey pine swayed dangerously and then plummeted, its fall making the ground shudder. A day's work was over. The big hands swung the axe into the fallen tree and left it there until morning. Tahoe City was less than three miles, and his throat needed to be washed free of dust. The evening sun was still warm as he swung his leg over his horse. The big appaloosa danced sideways as the big man's weight landed in the saddle. Stewart, in no great hurry, rode toward town.

It was always a possibility the boys' friendly evening drink together might be interrupted by the big man. If they were lucky, Stewart would choose one of the other saloons in town. The customers of Campbell's Custom House were unlucky that evening. The bar was busy and noisy. No one heard his footsteps. Only those closest to the swinging doors were aware who had just pushed them open, but there was a tangible reaction that spread within seconds. All talk started to peter out, and within seconds the silence was complete. Some locals downed their drinks, while others just abandoned theirs and left. The big man smiled a singularly unfriendly smile, as the last customer gave Stewart an exaggerated wide berth on his way out. A matter of a few minutes, and he had the whole saloon to himself.

Wishing he could do otherwise, the young bartender, Freddie Scott, stood his ground. Nervously the young man placed a bottle and glass on the bar counter. The big ham fist enveloped the bottle from neck to bottom. While Jim Stewart drank, Freddie started to clear up after the departed customers. Having poured and swallowed several glasses, Stewart wiped his mouth with the back of his hand. As Freddie moved back behind the bar, the big man fixed the young bartender with a stare.

"YOU. Didn't I already kill you, boy?" Stewart demanded of Scott.

"No, sir, you must be mistaken," Scott answered in a voice slightly higher than usual.

"Don't smart-mouth me, boy!"

It was useless, Freddie was trapped. Not even by admitting to his own death could he have avoided trouble.

"Got a gun, boy?"

"Mister Stewart, sir, please, I don't want no trouble."

As the young bartender pleaded for his life, two would-be customers walked into the saloon, cheerfully talking to each other, unaware of the lack of customers or the reason why. Stewart whirled around and noisily clamped a hand on his gun butt. The quickness of the action startled the two intruders into realizing the dire situation they had unwittingly walked in on. They slowly inched backward to the doors. Once outside, they decided to run. The big man followed as far as the swinging doors and watched their flight down the boardwalk. Laughing to himself, Stewart turned around and went back into the saloon.

His laugh died somewhere deep within him and his mouth fell open stupefied. He was looking down two shotgun barrels, the wrong way. Stewart went for his gun, but before he could reach it he was hurled back through the swinging doors. The big man's dead body crumpled on the deck outside. Freddie Scott, no expert with a rifle, had grimaced as he pulled the trigger. The recoil had knocked him to the ground. Hitting his head against a table as he fell, the young bartender had knocked himself unconscious.

When Scott came to his senses, the saloon was crowded. Upon hearing shots, some of the locals had braved the danger to find out who had been Stewart's latest victim. When the cry went out that it was indeed Stewart that was dead, all the others saloons emptied. A dazed Freddie Scott rubbing his bruised head looked up to a sea of faces. Toothless Larry Morgan asked him, "Did you shoot Stewart, Freddie?"

"Yes," answered Scott still dazed.

"Lordy, lordy, lordy! Young Freddie killed Jimmy Stewart!" Morgan gleefully shouted, barely able to keep his chewing tobacco from dribbling out of his toothless grin. A cheer reverberated around the packed saloon. "Fetch the judge, this has gotta be done lawful!" Morgan winked at the bewildered Scott. Pulling the young bartender to his feet, Morgan told him, "We're going to try you, but before the judge arrives, better be sure I have something to drink!"

The judge, a small man, moved with difficulty through the crowd. Upon instruction from Morgan, he clambered up onto the bar and addressed the attentive throng.

"This here is a court of law, and I am presiding judge for Placer County and the glorious state of California. All here shall show due reverence and be silent while the court debates the seriousness of this matter."

"Get on with it, judge, this ain't no lynching!" called a voice from the back.

"OK, enough of that!" the judge countered. "Get the defendant a chair!" Freddie was hurriedly sat down.

"Where is the arresting officer?" the judge asked.

"Ain't no arresting officer, Judge, we thought we cut all that malarkey out. Freddie's got to be back at work in a couple of minutes." Morgan sheepishly grinned at the judge.

"Look, Morgan, this has got to have some semblance of procedure," complained the judge.

There were murmurs, which got louder as the crowd started to get restless. The majority just wanted the judge to declare Freddie innocent. Morgan feared that they might lose the judge if an immediate compromise was not reached.

"Everyone here respects you, Judge, don't we, boys?"

Morgan turned around and stared hard at all the men in the room. No one said anything for a moment. Then, at Morgan's urging, there was mumbled approval.

Satisfied, the judge turned to Morgan. "Choose twelve men who can act as a jury and have them stand to the side." Morgan looked at the throng of men in front of him, nearly all of whom wanted to volunteer. Morgan eventually chose eleven men and appointed himself foreman. During the process, the noise level had risen again. The judge again asked for silence, Morgan turned to the men and put an erect finger to his lips.

"How do you plead to the killing of Jim Stewart?" The judge questioned the young bartender.

Scott was unsure what to say. He nervously looked at his sweaty palms and, in a quiet voice, resigned himself to his fate. "I guess...I'm guilty!' There was an audible groan from his audience.

"Freddie, were you provoked?" asked the judge.

Freddie looked puzzled.

"Did Jim Stewart threaten you?" continued the judge.

"He asked me if I had a gun." Freddie shuddered as he recalled the look on Jim Stewart's face.

"Were you scared, Freddie?" The judge did his best not to lead the uncomfortable defendant.

"Who's not scared of Big Jim Stewart?" Freddie exclaimed.

The judge was sure of the young man's innocence but he needed to coax the right response. "Freddie, did you feel threatened?" continued the judge.

"Yes, I did!"

The judge smiled a little having finally got the right answer.

"Then what did you do, Freddie?"

"I got the owner's rifle from the store room when Mr. Stewart chased a couple of men out of the bar." A feeling of emotion started to build up inside Freddie. With tears in his eyes he cried, "I didn't want to kill him but he went for his gun!" Those nearest to Scott gave him a sympathetic pat on the shoulder, and the judge breathed a sigh of relief.

"So, how do you plead, Freddie?" The judge's voice was softer and kinder. Raising his eye-brows and tilting his head to one side, the judge willed the young man to declare his innocence.

Not sure again of what he should say, Freddie looked at the judge for help. "Not guilty?"

The judge clasped his hand to his mouth. Not wishing to blatantly give the impression of leading the defendant, the judge gently nodded his head. There was evidence that the young man understood, as he wiped the tears from his face.

Caught up in the emotion of the moment, the judge cleared his own throat with a cough or two, and in a clear strong voice said, "Defendant Freddie Scott, how do you plead to the killing of Jim Stewart, guilty or not guilty?"

"Not guilty your honor!" There were cheers from the assembly.

The judge turned to Morgan and his men. "Members of the jury, you will go away and deliberate your verdict!" Morgan was just about to speak when the judge cut him off. "You WILL deliberate your verdict!" Morgan looked confused, but again before he could talk, the judge defiantly repeated, "You will GO AWAY and deliberate your verdict!"

Out of the corner of his mouth the bewildered Morgan asked in a quiet voice, "For how long?"

Under his breath the judge replied, "For at least five minutes."

Morgan ushered his men out of the swinging doors. Big Jim Stewart's body had already been removed. "Nice evening, aren't it?" Morgan commented. The evening air was very still. The few clouds above glowed pink and red which reflected on the surface of a motionless lake as the sunrays faded behind the western mountains. The other eleven had to agree that it was indeed a beautiful evening, but they were a little confused, just as Morgan had been earlier.

"What are we doing out here?" asked one of the eleven.

"Well, the judge, he likes to do everything proper, so we gotta give the impression that we are thinking whether Freddie told the truth or not."

Exasperated, one of the others expressed his annoyance. "We don't need to do that, we all know Jim Stewart for what he was!"

"Downright bully!" chipped in another.

"Yes, but the judge likes it done proper!"

"Waste of drinking time!" added another.

"That it may well be, but we aren't going to upset the judge anymore. So let's just stay out here another couple of minutes more and then go in!"

Morgan led the men back in a few minutes later.

The judge didn't need to hush the crowd, because everyone stopped talking, as the twelve men made their way back to the bar.

Once they were duly lined up, the judge addressed them.

"Has the jury reached their verdict?"

"We have your honor."

The judge turned to Freddie Scott. "The defendant will be upstanding." Young Freddie got to his feet and waited. The judge turned back to the jury.

"Is the verdict you have reached, the opinion of you all?"

Morgan turned to the rest of the jury. All eleven nodded in agreement. "It is your honor!"

"And what is the verdict of you all?"

"After very careful consideration, mind you," Morgan winked at the judge, "and lots of deliberation, as well," Morgan gave the judge another wink, "we, the jury, find the defendant, not guilty!"

The audience burst out cheering. The judge permitted the cheering for a while and then shouted, "Silence in court!" A shushing sound was audible from nearly everyone and the room was quiet again.

"Freddie Scott, you have been found not guilty by your peers, and therefore you are now free to go about your business. And your first business is to serve your judge and then your jury a drink!"

Remembering the Rough Ride of the Tribune 1877,(Hank and Horace 1859)

Definition of tribune: "A guardian appointed to defend the rights of the plebeians from the patricians. "

The Silver Dollar Saloon in Carson City was warm and noisy and reeked of tobacco and stale beer. A small band of musicians was playing while four ladies on stage picked up their skirts and kicked their gartered legs as high as they could! The girls missed a step or two, but these dancers were not the professionals that you would find in New York or Chicago. For all that, the on-looking men stamped their feet, clapped their hands, and whistled their appreciation. One whiskered man at the bar grinned from ear to ear. He had been steadily draining a bottle of whiskey for the past hour. His face was wrinkled by the summer sun and hardened by the winter winds. He had watery blue eyes, a prominent nose, and tobacco-stained teeth surrounded by a thick moustache and beard.

At the Silver Star Hotel across the road, several people were waiting for the westbound stage to take them up and over the Carson range of the Sierra on the way to Glenbrook. Everyone was getting a little impatient; the stage was already two hours late. It had been snowing all morning, and the frustrated hotel manager, David McGarrity, had used the weather as a convenient excuse. But the delay had nothing to do with weather. His frustration came from knowing that the stage was already in town and that the driver, Hank Monk, was drinking over at the Silver Dollar Saloon.

McGarrity was tolerant of Monk's drinking and for good reason. Hank Monk was just mad enough to drive a stage and team over the Sierra in any kind of weather. Monk was in the habit of drinking and driving; a bottle always kept him company while he fought the elements and negotiated his team over one of the worst trails in the West. Drunk or not, Hank Monk was held in high esteem by many who traveled over the mountains. When Monk came up behind a slow-moving wagon, the wagons pulled over to let him pass.

Toleration of Monk's drinking was not to be confused with approval, and it was David McGarrity's duty to get the passengers boarded without them meeting their drunken stagecoach driver.

With his frustration mounting, McGarrity excused himself from the passengers and marched over to the saloon. Inside the saloon McGarrity found Monk with his arm draped around a drinking buddy, and his free hand firmly wrapped around the neck of a nearly empty bottle. On seeing McGarrity he beamed a smile and confessed he had stopped by for one small tipple! Looking at the bottle, McGarrity asked how long had the tipple taken.

"I have been here barely five minutes!" lied Monk. He turned to his drinking buddy. "Isn't that right, Gordon?"

"Oh yes," replied his drunken friend. "Barely five minutes he's been stood here. He was stood over there before that."

"But I am as sober as an undertaker," declared Monk.

Gordon looked whimsical. "As sober as any undertaker I'll ever see alive!"

"Well, the undertaker can bury his last drink and he can get the stage rolling." McGarrity folded his arms while his incorrigible friend put the bottle to his lips and finished it. Monk then slapped Gordon on the back and staggered out in to the street.

While Monk found his way to Benton's Livery Stable, McGarrity returned to the five men and one lady waiting at the hotel. "Lady and gentlemen, if you would like to get ready, I think the stage will be here shortly!" There were a few comments from the passengers, most of which were about the fact it was snowing. "There will be extra blankets for your comfort, and the windows of the coach have flaps, so there is no need for any snow to get inside. Your driver is busy fitting the runners onto the stage."

"What are runners?" inquired one passenger.

"They are like wooden sleds fixed to the wheels. They are most ingenious! The stage just glides through the snow ..... and, of course, your driver is a master in these kinds of conditions."

"But isn't the pass dangerous in this kind of weather?" the lady suggested.

"Well, you should get over to Glenbrook before dark," McGarrity went on. "Your driver will decide what is safest."

"Are you talking about that old scoundrel, Hank Monk?" asked a man standing near the door. McGarrity looked a bit sheepish; Monk's reputation was no secret, but to his surprise the passenger followed up with a compliment. "Aye, I have been fortunate to have been his passenger before. He is a scallywag but a masterful handler of a team and coach."

"Yes, indeed. Known throughout the West for his love of whiskey," replied another man seated by the fire. "He's no respecter of persons, he treats everyone the same....... as Horace Greeley found out, to his chagrin."

"Yup, I have heard that story too, but I never knew the truth of it," interjected another male passenger.

Back in the stable, Monk already had the runners fitted, but he was having a little difficulty getting his team in order. Josh, the stable hand, was helping out but not to Monk's satisfaction.

"You can't put Agnes as a lead, she is too temperamental. And because she can't abide heights we'll put her in at number three. She'll know where the edge of the trail is better than me; my eyes aren't so good anymore. Put Drake in at number one, and make Major number two. Then put Hickory alongside Agnes at number four." We'll tie Sebastian off on the back Josh, just in case we run into any trouble and we need four extra legs."

Josh led out a large palomino already saddled and tied him to the back of the coach.

Monk went up to Drake and patted his large head.

"It's going to be nasty out there today, me handsome. You best be having a drop of warmth."

Monk poured some whiskey into a pail and gave it to the horse; the stable boy looked on in astonishment as Drake lapped it up. However, Monk did not share his whiskey with any of the other horses.

"What about the others?" the stable lad laughed.

"Horses don't like whiskey, Josh! Now Drake, he's a little more than just a horse. He was a Democrat in a previous life!" winked Monk.

Once the horses were realigned in the traces, Josh led the team out of the stable and into the half-light of a snowy midday.

McGarrity watched as the stage pulled up to the hotel. He dashed out ahead of the passengers. "Hank, please hide any bottles you have, the lady passenger is already nervous. You've got five gentlemen and one lady and quite a bit of luggage."

The passengers gathered their things and walked out to the stagecoach. Monk made a few tongue-in-cheek comments as he took some of the heavier bags up to the roof of the stage. McGarrity and the passengers caught a glimpse of a bottle in Monk's coat pocket. In response to David's look of thunder, Hank bowed his head and lifted his hands in phony apology.

He pulled the whiskey bottle out of his pocket and made a declaration to the passengers below. "OK, I promise not to touch a drop, if any of you would like to keep me company on top?"

The passengers looked at each other, but no one volunteered.

One of the passengers who knew Monk's reputation said, "Well, at least none of the horses are drunk!"

"Quite right, hardly any of them," Monk cajoled. "I'll keep the flaps up until we turn to go up the mountain; till that time you men can smoke, and lady too, if you've a mind to!"

McGarrity ensured that the lady sat in the middle and was well wrapped in blankets.

"Is it going to be safe, Mr. Monk?" asked the nervous lady.

"Well, Ma'am, I have talked to the horses and we are all agreed that it's going to be difficult but we are all determined. And they have told me as long as I keep singing they are going to do their very best for us. I just got to loosen my vocal chords with a little whiskey and we'll be in fine fettle." He gave her his best reassuring smile.

"Your horses talk to you, Mr. Monk?"

"All the time, Ma'am; if we didn't understand each other, I wouldn't be able to drive a stage."

The main street of Carson City had been lined with newly planted poplar trees, which became ever more ghostly as the weather closed in. There were two or three brave souls still out on the street, but no one was out for just a leisurely stroll. Most of the townspeople were in their homes or in the half-dozen saloons on Main Street.

Monk flicked his whip above the heads of the team and the stage jerked. The horses' strength freed the runners from their icy grip and soon they were into an effortless canter.

The stage made surprising progress as bits of snow and ice flew up behind the rear axle. The passengers sat back and hoped the journey wouldn't be too arduous.

Some three miles out of town, Monk could see a lone rider approaching from the west, frantically waving his hand. Monk stopped the coach, and, while waiting for the rider to get closer, he extracted the bottle of whiskey from his pocket and took a couple of healthy swallows. The passengers were vaguely aware Monk was talking to someone outside but what was being said was lost in the noise of the storm. The next thing they knew, Monk came to the stage door. The passengers were bemused to see their stagecoach driver, he looked like an old man, as his moustache, his beard, and his even eyebrows were caked in snow.

"We have a problem," Monk shouted above the noise of the wind. "There's been an avalanche on Kings Canyon and the trail is blocked. It won't be cleared until the weather improves. We could go on to Genoa and take the Kingsbury Grade but that would be slow going in this kind of weather. By the time we got up the east shore to Glenbrook, it would be well after dark and the horses will be exhausted."

"Do we have to go to Glenbrook, Mr. Monk?" asked one of the male passengers.

Again Monk shouted above the storm. "Well Benton's has arranged your rooms at the Tahoe House, and that is where the new team of horses is waiting for us. I can't be sure of finding a new team elsewhere, and you have no rooms booked on south shore."

"What is your suggestion, Mr. Monk?" asked the lady.

"Well, my habit is to get people where they are going, but with a lady on board I am not going to be foolish. I suggest we get out of the storm and go back to Carson, where I know you will be safe and warm. If Kings Canyon is still blocked tomorrow, maybe we can arrange a change of horses on south shore."

There was a resigned agreement among the passengers and so the stage went back to Carson City. Once back at the Silver Star Hotel, David McGarrity hurriedly got the rooms ready for those that needed them. Two of the passengers who lived locally returned home.

As Monk helped with the luggage, the lady asked him in front of the other hotel guests if he would tell the story of his famous ride with Horace Greeley. Monk excused himself and said he hadn't told the story for many years.

McGarrity jumped in and said, "You know, Hank, I have never heard your version of that story either."

"Well it was a longtime ago, and I am happy to let it be."

McGarrity turned to the lady. "Have you seen Mr. Monk's gold watch, Ma'am? He was given it by the most distinguished residents of Nevada, in memory of that day. Whether you like it or not, Hank, that day has gone down in the annals of western folklore. I think these people deserve to hear the story from your own lips, since today you broke your habit of getting people to where they are going."

"Well, that's hardly fair," grumbled Monk. "I can't control avalanches."

"That's very true, but you know what I discovered from Ted Herman, who stopped you today? He told me that the avalanche happened barely an hour before he stopped you. So, you know what that means?"

Monk was a bit lost in thought and for words. "No, what?"

"It means if the stage had been on time today, you would have been on the other side of that avalanche, and right now you would have been in Glenbrook."

A hurt look came over Monk's face. He looked around at the half-dozen faces gathered before him. "Had to get those runners on, and had a little bit of difficulty."

McGarrity raised an eyebrow, knowing the real reason why the stage was late.

"You know, Hank, not only do these people deserve to hear your story, but I deserve it too!"

Monk was red faced with embarrassment. Yes, McGarrity did deserve it and he was struck to the core, thinking that maybe he had let his friend down once too often.

"You really want to hear that old story?" he said, looking again at the expectant faces. No one said a word, but several of them nodded. Monk looked at his pocket-watch. "OK, I am first going to the saloon to get myself a drink, and I'll be back by seven. I want Josh to be here too." Monk had a real softness for the fifteen-year-old stable lad, who always helped him to get ready. "I am going to tell this story because I am indeed indebted to David. I will tell it because perhaps I did let my passengers down today. And finally I will tell it so Josh can take this old story into a new century."

Without another word Monk marched out of the hotel, got back on the driver's box, and drove the stage to the livery stable.

It was fifteen minutes past the hour when McGarrity walked over to the saloon. There was Monk with his friend Gordon again, merrily drinking and laughing. McGarrity reminded Monk that he had promised to tell the Greeley story back at the hotel.

Monk turned to his drinking friend Gordon. "I got to go to the hotel and tell the Greeley story."

"Do you even remember the Greeley, story Hank?" Gordon inquired.

"Why you drunken old fool I remember it as if it was yesterday."

"But Hank you DON'T remember yesterday!"

"Look, you old fool….," Monk turned on his friend with a bit of annoyance. "Josh is going to be there. The lad wasn't born when Greeley was here. I want the lad to remember me and remember me telling the story. You and I, Gordon, we won't see the twentieth century, but Josh will."

"I am off to tell that story, probably for the last time, and I want it to be good."

Gordon smiled at his old friend. "Go tell it, my friend, and I won't be there to embarrass you when you say something I've never heard before."

It was still snowing as Monk and McGarrity trudged over to the hotel. There were maybe twenty people in the lobby, including young Josh. A seat had been left vacant to the side of a roaring log fire. McGarrity whispered to his friend "The seat is for you Mr. Monk."

Hank turned to look at his friend who addressed him with such deference.

"It's been a great joy to know you, Hank."

Humbled by his friend's respect, Hank took his seat. He noticed a glass of whiskey had been placed on the table in front of him. "First of all," Monk grabbed the glass and lifted it to his mouth, "I aren't anyone special."

"I heard you could turn a stagecoach around at full gallop on a city street," exclaimed an excited voice.

"Never done such a thing, as I remember," replied the stagecoach driver. "Seems like such a silly thing to do."

"Wait a minute, didn't I hear of you once spending a winter's night on Spooner Summit, Mr. Monk?"

"Yes, that I did, but that was because I unknowingly drove a stage onto a frozen mill pond covered in snow and the stage broke through the ice. Up to my thighs in ice-cold water, now that's something you don't easily forget. We didn't get the stage out of the pond until the spring." Monk laughed.

"Are you not known as the Knight of the Lash?" asked another.

"It was dear old Horace who gave me that nickname, that day in '59."

A look of nostalgia was evident on the stage driver's weathered face as he remembered Horace with some affection.

"I heard that you cost Horace Greeley the presidential election in '72," interrupted another.

Monk's eyebrows knotted together as his expression changed. "How can that be?"

"It was said the story of his stagecoach ride to Placerville was told on Capitol Hill, to ridicule Greeley on the floor of the Senate."

Monk wanted to refute that he had any dealings with sabotaging Greeley's presidential run. "Horace wasn't always liked. He stood for things, he fought against corruption, and he didn't stay dumb, like the most of us. He knew the worst of those political charlatans, and his enemies wanted any nonsense to make him look foolish. If they chose a harmless incident which involved me several years earlier, it just shows how desperate they were."

"So, Mr. Monk, you didn't purposely set out to embarrass him that day?"

"For heaven's sake, no. I had a bit of fun with him, that's all."

"Can you tell us your own version?"

Monk looked up to see the hopeful face of the young lady.

"Well, you have to remember it was a long time ago, more than eighteen years now. Before the Civil War, before Lincoln was president, before Reno came into existence, before the railroad, before the Indian troubles, before the Pony Express, and before the Kingsbury Grade. The West was a different place. For a start, this wasn't Nevada back then; this was Mormon Utah Territory, and the governor was Brigham Young. Most of the Mormons had gone back to Salt Lake City by '57, and those of us left here on the western side of the territory wanted to break free from Salt Lake City. Carson City was a community of no more than three dozen buildings. Lake Tahoe was known as Lake Bigler and barely a handful of people lived on the south shore of the lake. The main route over the mountains then was via Diamond Valley. Virginia City was just a few tents, and all the millionaires had yet to be made. There was no timber cutting, no wooden v-flumes, no lumber yards, and no telegraph on the eastern side of the Sierra."

The atmosphere in the hotel lobby was palpable, as if all those gathered were in the presence of living history. The story was well known in many variations through-out the country, but they were to hear the story from the only man living who was actually there.

"Of course, I was different too. I could drive all day and night when I was young. I perhaps took risks I shouldn't have done, but when you are caught up in a spirit of an age, when everything is new, when every day brought change, you didn't live by rules. You had to make things happen. Fred Taylor, he made things happen. He built the first hotel in Carson and defiantly called it The Nevadan; he knew even back then that someday Nevada would be born.

One bright summer morning he hung a big sign on his hotel. It said, "Horace Greeley will stay here tonight." It was partly because of that sign and how all the towns-people were talking about Horace that got me a little bent out of shape. I was a little bit of a rebel back then."

McGarrity, who was leaning against the back wall, started laughing. "You do yourself a disservice my friend. You are still the rebel."

"Maybe that's so, but I feel sorry for Horace now, God rest his soul, and just maybe I was a little naughty. Horace Greeley was a popular man back then, before those political hacks played with his reputation. Horace Greeley was probably the most important easterner ever to come out west. You know he personally met the crowned heads of Europe. Why, he was even thrown into jail in Paris. Horace was all right. I might just have been a little in awe of him, but I was determined I weren't gonna let it show. Everybody wanted to meet him, but I pretended I didn't care."

"It was July, and it was very hot and dusty the day we met. I had been drinking a bit the night before and if my memory serves me right I was a little bit late that day too…"

 *Hank and Horace, 1859*

Besides the sign hanging outside the Nevadan hotel, leaflets had been distributed through the surrounding areas: *"Horace Greeley, the founder and editor of the New York Tribune, an ex-United States congressman and possible future presidential candidate, has come to discover the West, so please welcome him to Carson City, the future capital of the new Nevada Territory."*

Thus it was that Greeley was welcomed by all the inhabitants of Carson City, except the one man who was scheduled to take him into California. In Salt Lake City, the newspaper man had been given a rare interview by the famous Mormon leader Brigham Young. That had been eight days and five hundred miles earlier, and he still wasn't out of Utah Territory. Now he was finally on the western fringe of the territory on the border of California, in a small community which had grown up around a desert trading post known as Eagle Station and which had been recently renamed Carson City.

This high desert outpost was his last stop before going into the Golden State. The next day he would take an early-morning stage across the Sierra Nevada Mountains. He would see Yosemite, San Francisco, and the Pacific Ocean. Tomorrow night he was to deliver an important speech to the gold-mining community of Placerville, in the foothills above Sacramento. The stage he had taken from Salt Lake had headed back to the Mormon capital. It was to be a new stage and a new driver that would take him into California. After

Yosemite he would take a paddle steamer from Sacramento down the delta to the San Francisco Bay, so he had just a little more than two hundred miles of rattling around in a stage.

Small as the desert community was, there was a constant coming and going of wagons. It seemed there had been a valuable discovery of silver, as well as gold, in the hills to the northeast. Dozens of miners were headed there to try their luck. Still, the distinguished visitor was creating a lot of excitement of his own.

Once washed, Greeley decided to wander along the small town's boardwalk; several people stopped him to shake hands. The last rays of the setting sun reflected pink and purple in the wispy clouds overhead and a warm breeze blew through the valley. Greeley had been given the royal treatment wherever he had gone, and people flocked from far and wide to see the great man. As he wandered around the small community, he smelled the fragrance of the sagebrush and heard the sweet sound of a harmonica played by a solitary figure leaning on the fence of a nearby corral.

Inside the town's only saloon the Golden Nugget, a small group of men were drinking and playing cards. One of those in the saloon that night was the thirty-one-year-old Hank Monk. The young stagecoach driver had a moustache but no beard back then. He, like Greeley, was from New York, but from the opposite end of the Empire State. The two men had never met before, but that was all going to change in the next twenty-four hours.

In keeping with the preferential treatment he had been accustomed to, Greeley was going to be the only passenger on an exclusive overland stage to California. Fred Taylor had made all the arrangements for his distinguished guest. The newspaper man had been given a lavish breakfast, and after packing his things he was down in the hotel lobby waiting for his special ride west. The stage was already more than thirty minutes late and Taylor was getting nervous. He took leave from the great man's company and decided to go over to the livery stable, where the stage was kept. Toby, the stable lad, had everything ready; the four horses were coupled together and it was just the driver who was missing.

"Where's Monk?" Taylor asked.

The stable lad shrugged his shoulders.

"Go to his lodgings and get him down here as quickly as possible!"

Toby ran around to the boarding house where Monk usually stayed when he was in town, but there was no sign of him.

Frustrated by Toby's news, Taylor murmured to himself, "He was definitely in town yesterday."

Back at the hotel, Greeley had also started to become a little concerned. He was supposed to deliver his speech to the Placerville community at seven o'clock that evening and there were more than a hundred miles of trail to cover. Even if they left straightaway it would be tight.

Taylor had a sneaking suspicion where Monk might be; he crossed the road to the Golden Nugget. There, crumpled in a dark corner of the saloon, snoring quietly was Monk, oblivious to the world around him. It was too late to get a replacement driver; Taylor would somehow have to get Monk sober and ready.

"Wake up, you scoundrel! Please, Hank, wake up!"

Immediately one of Monk's eyes shot open, while the other slept on. "Leave me alone... another hour or two."

"You are already late. Please, Hank, this is my reputation as well as yours." Taylor's tone was desperate. "It's Greeley, the most important passenger you've ever had. Come on, please wake up and get going."

On realizing it was Taylor who was pleading with him, Monk smiled and told his friend not to worry.

"Hank, you are already an hour late, how can I not worry?"

Monk now had both eyes half opened. "What's all the fuss about? Horace is a New Yorker, I am a New Yorker. Nothing special about us; we all fall over when we're drunk."

"That's just it, Hank, Greeley doesn't drink and he won't understand you, even though you're from New York. And I don't think you should be calling him Horace either."

"Fuss and nonsense; he puts his britches on one leg at a time, just like we all do! When's Horace got to be at Lake's Crossing?"

"Hank, he's going to Placerville — Placerville in California!"

"When's he got to be in Hangtown then?" Monk used the nickname that Placerville was often known by.

"He's got to be there by seven o'clock this evening."

"What time is it now?"

"It's just after nine."

"Well, he ought to get going, otherwise he won't make it!"

"Listen, you drunken fool, YOU are taking him to Placer-ville, and YOU have got to take him there. Please, Hank, for me!"

"OK, OK, I'll do it for you, but not for Horace. Give me five minutes, got to get the team ready."

"Toby has everything ready; we are all waiting on you."

Monk hoisted himself to his feet, "Got to get my supplies."

"What supplies?"

"Well, I aren't driving all the way to Hangtown without some liquid refreshment."

"Please, Hank, don't let Greeley see you with any whiskey."

"I am always the soul of discretion my friend." Monk put a knowing finger to the side of his nostril. "You just get your all-important passenger ready for the quickest mountain ride ever."

Taylor returned to the hotel and told Horace Greeley that the driver had encountered a little difficulty but would be with them soon. Greeley asked whether it was still possible to get over to Placerville in time. Taylor told Greeley that Hank Monk was the best stagecoach driver in the West and if anyone could do it, then Monk was the driver who could.

Before leaving the saloon, Monk grabbed a couple bottles of whiskey and chalked it up on the board behind the bar. He looked at himself in the saloon's mirror and straightened his wrinkled clothes as best he could. He palmed his disheveled hair into some sort of obedience and went to where the stage and team were waiting.

Having checked the stage, Monk patted the broad face of a grey that was in harness with another three horses. "Well boys, we have an important man from the east to deliver across the mountains." Satisfied that all was ready, Monk drove the stage to the hotel.

Taylor watched from the hotel's window. On seeing the stage, he walked out with Mr. Greeley's bag and a few seconds later the great man appeared himself. There were a dozen or so well-wishers wanting to say goodbye.

Taylor then turned to his guest. "Mr. Greeley, I want you to meet Hank Monk, your driver."

Slowly realizing that Taylor wanted him to shake Greeley's hand, Monk got down from the driver's box.

"Mr. Monk, it is a pleasure. I hope we can get to Placerville on time?"

"Horace," Monk addressed Greeley as if he had known him all his life, "I have made a promise to all the saints hereabout to deliver you one way or another to Hangtown, and there aren't gonna be much to stop me!"

The locals smiled, as they knew pretty much what that meant coming from the likes of Monk. Monk pulled out a whiskey bottle and offered a drink to his smartly dressed passenger. Taylor looked up to the heavens and shook his head.

Greeley noticed Taylor's pained look. "I don't think so, Mr. Monk. I need to keep a clear head."

Greeley thanked Taylor and the others for their hospitality. Looking over the top of his spectacles, he turned to the hotel manager and spoke softly, "Quite a character your Mr. Monk."

Taylor assured him that Monk was the finest driver in the territory and no one knew the mountain passes better. Greeley had to bow to Taylor's better knowledge of the man.

Having shaken the hands of the locals, Greeley turned around to get on the stage. Monk, who had yet to get back on board himself, said to his only passenger, "If I may be permitted, I'd like to introduce you to all the team." Taylor shot his friend a look of disgust, but Monk continued on, laying a hand on the first horse. "This is the noble Sir Regis, who was sired from the Scot Greys that fought at the battle of Waterloo. Monk moved around to each horse in turn. This is Tyrone, who was bred from the horse which Meriwether Lewis rode west. This is Prince, who once belonged to Davy Crockett. And last but not least, this is Running Star, who was stolen from the Shoshone Indians, and they very much want him back!"

"And you? Who are you, Mr. Monk?" Greeley inquired.

"I am a son of an innkeeper from Waddington, New York. I believe we are related to royalty, but we are waiting for our confirmation from Queen Victoria. Until then my lot in life is to be a humble servant. I am here to serve his eminence and to take him, and his blue parasol, on his journey west."

"It's not a parasol, Mr. Monk, it's an umbrella."

"Well, it would have been more useful if it had been a parasol, because it don't rain here, at least ways not at this time of the year."

"Well, I think it's time we left, Mr. Monk. If we cannot make Placerville in time, I think they have a telegraph wire connection at the relay station in Strawberry."

Monk knew Greeley doubted his ability to make an on time arrival happen and Taylor knew this was like waving a red flag to a bull; Monk never took kindly to being underestimated.

"OK, Horace, if you would like to get your honorable personage aboard your exclusive charabanc, we'll get going. If you need to talk to me at any time, you can use the hatch above your head." Monk pointed to a foot-square hole in the ceiling of the coach.

As Greeley got inside, Monk clambered up to the driver's box. In sight of Taylor, the brazen Monk took a healthy swig from one of his bottles and took hold of the reins. He shook the reins, the horses responded and the stage started in motion. The locals waved as the easterner, satisfied he was finally on his way, waved goodbye from the stage window. The stage ambled along for twenty minutes or more but not at the urgent pace that Greeley thought was necessary.

"Do you think we can go a little faster, Mr. Monk?" Not sure Hank had heard, Greeley repeated himself.

"I just want ALL your admirers to be able to see you as you go by, Horace."

"There is nothing but sagebrush outside, Mr. Monk."

"Well, we have the smartest jackrabbits in all the country out here, and they shouldn't be deprived a glimpse of their future president." Changing the subject completely, Monk suggested. "You know, Horace, you ought to interview Snow-shoe Thompson when we get to Woodfords. Now there's a real local hero."

Still, the stage ambled on at a leisurely rate.

"Mr. Monk, please can we move a little faster?"

Pretending not to have heard, Monk continued, "Delivers the mail over the mountains in the snow, he does, on two pieces of whittled-wood."

Through the hatch, Greeley caught sight of Monk taking a swallow from a bottle.

"Why do you drink so much, Mr. Monk?"

"Because of the bugs I swallow, Horace. Have to wash them down and make sure they are all drowned."

It was nearly two o'clock when the stage slowly came into Woodfords Station. They had barely covered thirty-five miles in four and a half hours; at this rate Greeley doubted they would even make Strawberry by seven. He had started to wonder why Fred Taylor had sung Monk's praises so highly.

At Woodfords, a new team of horses were put in the traces and Greeley was anxious to go as soon as everything was ready. Monk said, "Let me introduce you to your new team, Horace."

"Please, Mr. Monk, I have no wish to be introduced to any more blue-blooded equine. That you yourself are royalty is enough for me. Can we PLEASE go on our way and a little faster, Mr. Monk? This is a very important meeting in Placerville, and the whole community is expecting me."

Greeley got back into the stage. Monk, disappointed he could not introduce his new team, clambered back on top of the driver's box. Again they were in motion, but again it was at a slow pace.

"Would you like me to stop on the way and give you a view of Lake Bigler, Horace?"

"No thank you, Mr. Monk. When I am back this way, I would love you to take me on a slow leisurely stage ride and show me all the sights and introduce me to Mr. Thompson and others, but not this time, and definitely not today."

A few miles out from Woodfords, a buck-board driven by an elderly lady overtook the stage. Frustrated, Greeley shouted up to his hard-of-hearing driver, "You're being very tiresome, Mr. Monk!"

"Me? I'm not tired any, Horace. I had a good sleep on the saloon floor."

"If I have insulted you, Mr. Monk, can you please forgive me? If you get me to Placerville on time, I will buy you a new suit of clothes."

"Bribery is it, Horace? You're a politician if ever I met one. I promised Fred I'd get you to Hangtown, and get you to Hangtown I will."

Suddenly, Monk let out a loud cry and the stage lurched violently. Greeley was thrown backward against his seat. He looked out of the stage window to see the surrounding countryside hurtling by. The horses were in a full gallop, and the speeding stage swerved dangerously around the buckboard that had passed them several minutes earlier. The startled lady driver coughed as the dust flew heavily about her. Inside, Horace desperately tried to grab hold of anything to stop being bounced up and down.

"The wind has shifted direction, Horace." Monk gleefully announced. "We'll make good use of it over the mountain."

Greeley could not keep his seat as the stage careened around every bend in the trail. He was slammed against every hard surface inside the stage. Every time Greeley opened his mouth to speak, he was thrown from one side to the other. He suffered it a little longer before pleading with his driver.

"Please, Mr. Monk, forget about arriving in Placerville at seven, just slow down!"

"You just keep your seat, Horace. We've got a tail wind now and we'll be even faster on the down slope."

"God forbid, I won't be any good black and blue! The meeting isn't that important."

"I won't hear of it, Horace, Your public awaits you and my duty is to get you to them."

The stage sped all the way to Strawberry, and Horace was relieved for the stage to stop again. It was just before four o'clock, and they had gotten over the mountains and were well on the downward stretch. They had covered the last thirty miles in less than two hours. Greeley was now not in a hurry to go on.

At Strawberry another new team was put in the traces. Monk had not gotten down from the driver's box at any time. After taking some refreshment, Greeley was slow in coming out of the station.

"What about our new team, Mr. Monk, who are they?"

Monk smiled at the newspaper man. "You know, Horace, I am beginning to like you. I am afraid I am not familiar with any of these horses, but they all look pretty stouthearted to me."

"Mr. Monk, you are my erstwhile friend. All I desire in this world right now is for you to like me and to give me the most comfortable of rides the rest of the way."

"Are you sure you don't want to send your telegram?" chided Monk.

"I have no intention of sending that telegram, as you well know."

"Well, my friend, if you feel no need to send that telegram and with the wind behind us as it has been since we left Woodfords, I think we don't have to drive quite as fast. So, get inside and we'll get you down to Hangtown on time I think, just another forty miles to go."

"I am in your capable hands, Hank." Monk smiled at Greeley's use of his Christian name for the first time. In response to Monk's smile, Greeley continued, "I met Queen Victoria and Prince Albert in London. I'll write to the queen and suggest she makes you a knight of the realm. They'll call you 'the Knight of the Lash.'"

"Whether I become a knight or not, Horace, I will always wish you to call me Sir Hank.

Monk laughed and Greeley smiled for the first time since he had left Carson City.

"You know, Hank, you mentioned Sir Regis being sired from the Scot Greys at Waterloo. I also met the Duke of Wellington. I saw him at the Crystal Palace in Hyde Park….a truly magnificent construction of glass and iron, but it suffered from the problem of bird droppings. I believe it was the duke who suggested the use of sparrow hawks."

"Well, Horace, I could talk to you all day, but sadly we must press on."

"Remember, Sir Hank, those people in Placerville won't mind if I am thirty minutes late."

"A promise...is a promise, my friend and Hank Monk always makes good on his promises."

At first the pace out of Strawberry was not so fast and Horace was able to relax. It had been a day he would never forget, and Hank Monk was a man he would never forget either. It seemed Monk had timed the journey to the nth degree and the newspaper man had been taught a lesson by probably the wiliest, whiskey-filled stagecoach driver of all time.

Hank had indeed purposely played with Greeley, knowing all along that he would get to Placerville at exactly seven o'clock, but now there was an unforeseen difficulty. In Diamond Spring, a welcoming committee was gathered. Dozens of people, complete with marching band and military attachment, were set to escort the great man in a grand procession the last five miles into Placerville. Monk looked warily on the people he could see blocking the trail up ahead. All these people were going to delay him, and if they didn't get out of the way, he might not reach Placerville on time as he had promised.

"Hang on, Horace!" Monk shouted.

Suddenly the stage lurched a second time as it was again being driven at neck-break speed. The stage and horses flew down toward the gathering. The people in harm's way panicked as it became evident that the stage was not going to slow down. People pushed each other to get out of the way. Many of them fell over, and a base drum was hurriedly abandoned by one of the fleeing band members. As several horses' hooves and one of the stage wheels went over the drum, the stage bounced higher and harder than it had at any previous time. Greeley was thrown with so much force that his head went through the hatch, and for a moment he was stuck with his head protruding through the roof of the stage.

Several of those gathered shouted for Hank Monk to stop as the stage thundered through their midst, but Monk ignored all their pleas. He had made his promise and nothing would deter him from it.

As Monk pulled the stage up to the Cary House in Placerville, a look of horror was evident on the faces of those who had stayed behind to prepare the meeting. "Where are the mayor and all the townspeople who were supposed to meet you in Diamond Spring? Where is the marching band and the attachment who were supposed to escort you here?"

Greeley painfully got out of the coach. It was a totally inglorious way to end what had been one of the most humiliating days of his life. He was battered and bruised, his jacket was torn at the shoulder, his neck-tie had shifted to one side, and one of his spectacles was badly cracked. However, before he could muster enough strength to speak, his cheerful nemesis declared "Ten minutes early Horace!"

"And that's about how I remember it." Monk smiled at his delighted listeners inside the Silver Star lobby.

"If Horace Greeley was so important, why didn't you have a shotgun ride with you?" asked one of the men in the audience.

"Well, if there had been a shotgun rider with me, I would probably have lost him overboard by the time we left Woodfords." Monk laughed. "There was no need for a shotgun and I rarely had one. Of course, the Paiutes went on the warpath the year after Greeley's visit but I never had any real trouble with them. I used to give them whiskey, which I told them I made myself. They knew if they killed me, then that would be an end to their firewater."

"Really, Mr. Monk, you are one of the most unusual persons I have ever met," the delighted lady clapped gently. "So you drink in the winter to keep yourself warm while singing to your horses, and you drink in the summer because of the bugs and to appease the Indians?"

"All good reasons you have to admit Ma'am. I also drink in case I fall off the driver's box, which only hurts when I am sober."

 **(9) From Disaster to Triumph, 1906 - 1907**

The man at the end of Homewood pier was waiting for the Steamer Ship *Tahoe* to come around the point from Tahoe City. He was overweight and a bit sluggish on his feet, but this belied a natural aptitude he had in the water. No one could swim like Martin Lowe. He could dive more than sixty feet, retrieve any chosen item off the bottom of the lake, and bring it back up to the surface. Somehow, he had turned this talent to his advantage and had become a showman, performing aquatic feats for visiting holiday-makers. His shape and size gave his antics a comical edge, and even the locals would drop by to see the man they knew as "The Homewood Walrus."

Martin had come from obscurity a year earlier, a drifter who had arrived in the late spring of 1906 looking for work. He was originally employed as a handy man and often used to walk around with a hammer in hand. But what work he actually did, was an amusing mystery to the locals of Homewood. He hadn't received much scrutiny in those early days, and he had liked it that way. Now he was some kind of freakish tourist attraction, which he didn't mind either......... as long as he was rewarded!

In the spring of 1906, Martin Lowe's life had literally come crashing to an end. He was working as a house painter in San Francisco and had been renting a single room on Larkin Street.

On the evening of April 17th, he went to bed at nine thirty, only to be woken at eleven by the continual barking of a neighborhood dog. The dog never did stop barking, but Martin eventually drifted into a restless sleep. Then, before daybreak, he was suddenly tossed from his bed. Before he could completely come to his senses, an explosion flung him violently toward the street below.

Bruised, dazed, and bewildered, he slowly became aware that the house was missing its walls and ceiling. The air was full of dust and he sat there choking and spluttering, uncomfortably perched on the remnants of the house. As he had struggled to his feet, in his torn and shredded pajamas, the light of the coming day brought evidence of an unimaginable disaster. The explosion had been deafening. Every single house in the street was a shell of its original structure. As he took it all in, slowly his hearing recovered and the surreal turned into a dreadful reality. He remained motionless in the ruins of the house, listening to the sounds of horses whining and distant explosions, as the sun rose on the shambles of a broken city.

It was his first and only experience of being in an earthquake. Stunned, shocked, and dismayed, he struggled to his feet but a massive aftershock knocked him down again, and it took him a long time to trust the ground enough to stand once more. Caught between wanting to remain still and an urgent need to get away, he haphazardly searched through the rubble for some of his possessions. After an hour or so, he found some clothes, boots, a blanket, fourteen dollars, and his dead landlady. With these few possessions he spent the next few hours stumbling over the ruins of a devastated San Francisco. There were numerous aftershocks that brought renewed terror and palls of smoke which billowed into an ever-blackening cloud that hung low over the city for days.

There was also a pervasive smell of gas and the sound of people moaning wherever he went. Many people, still in their night attire, wandered aimlessly wanting to escape but fearful to leave their homes.

Martin kept on moving. He stepped over bits of masonry and all other kinds of debris in the streets. Some paved streets had cracked and buckled, crippling the cable car service and making all other means of transportation nearly impossible. Drivers abandoned their carriages, unhitched their horses, and left them to fend for themselves. Aftershocks would panic the horses, and one would occasionally bolt past the homeless house painter.

After precariously picking his way over a variety of obstacles, Martin turned a corner to see a jet of flame roaring from a hole in the sidewalk. It was just one of several ruptured gas mains below street level that would add to a growing inferno. He passed half and completely destroyed buildings, he witnessed several rescue attempts but a lot of people simply sat huddled together, whimpering. As night approached he saw soldiers with rifles and hastily written signs on damaged properties saying "Keep Out!"

He was making his way to Union Square when he was stopped by a fire so huge that it engulfed a city block. The heat was tremendous, and burning embers filled the sky and flew in all directions. There were no efforts to put the fire out, and it became obvious that soon many more blocks would go up in flames. He had to abandon all hope of reaching Union Square, so he turned around and headed to the waterfront.

The first night on the wharf was fine; there was even a sense of camaraderie, everyone being in the same boat. He spent an uncomfortable but relatively peaceful night on one of the many boardwalks with hundreds of other homeless victims. By afternoon of the second day a feeling of unease set in and several people had climbed the fences surrounding the piers to get at the store of goods unloaded from ships. By the second night, fires were deliberately set by looting, wayward gangs, and various disputes broke out.

He spent the second night with one eye open and had to move several times to avoid being robbed of his meager possessions. On the third afternoon, things went from bad to worse, as federal troops indiscriminately shot suspected looters. The innocent fell along with the guilty. Many people lay dead and dying, in a city that was ablaze for more than fifty blocks from Market Street to the harbor area to Van Ness Boulevard. Nothing in the legendary Wild West compared with the hellfire and insanity of those few days in San Francisco. All he thought to do was escape, to find somewhere he could think and be safe.

He fled the federal troops and found himself on a ferry over to Oakland. He might have stayed and seen the city rebuilt. There would, in time, be plenty of work for house painters. But this was a case of survival, and he chose to leave the mayhem behind him. From Oakland he took a train to Sacramento where he visited a cousin. After a week, he wore out his welcome and he decided to move on. He intended going over to Reno, but for some reason he got off the train at Truckee. From there he caught the train down the fourteen-mile spur through the Truckee River Canyon to Lake Tahoe. He had borrowed a little money from his cousin, but it was clear it would not have lasted very long, so he walked around the small town of Tahoe City looking for work. Someone told him there were summer cottages that had needed repair down in the small hamlet of Homewood, six miles outside of town.

It was the end of the first week of May when Lowe arrived in Homewood, on Lake Tahoe's west shore. At first his tales of the San Franciscan quake had generated both interest and sympathy, and he was hired to look after the maintenance of six holiday cottages near the Homewood pier. He was permitted to stay in one until the first holiday-makers arrived later in the season. On Tahoe's glorious west shore he felt he had found the peace to recuperate. He had always liked swimming, and, even though the lake's waters were cool; he spent every summer's day swimming for thirty minutes or more.

The lake had no undertow and the water was so clear that the bottom was visible more than a hundred yards off shore. During his summer swims, Martin retrieved several items lying in among the submerged rocks, stones and sand. They were mostly useless relics…….. bits of old canoes, buckets with holes, abandoned crawfish traps, pieces of old rope, broken life buoys, a shattered ship's lantern, an oar or two and other similar objects. However, nearer to the pier he found items of more value……..personal trinkets, lighters, spectacles, a bracelet, a snuff box, a scarf, a harmonica, etc. Anything of value he took back to his cottage.

One day he was seen coming out of the water looking at a pocket watch.

"What you got there?" asked a kindly stranger.

"Just something I found."

"Could belong to someone?"

"Well, if it did, it's mine now."

"Could be there's a reward for finding it?"

This revelation began the wheels turning which would lead Martin to purposely look for owners of lost property. He also retrieved objects at the request of people, which eventually led him to performing tricks for tourists. Martin received plaudits' from far and wide, and now he was the main attraction of a visit to Homewood.

It was a warm late afternoon as Martin waited for the steamer. Tired of standing on the pier, Martin sat down and swung his legs over the edge of the boardwalk. The *S.S. Tahoe* was later than usual. He watched the sunlight dance on the water as a young boy and his dog ran past. At the end of the pier, two fishermen were pulling in their lines after a moderately successful day. He had already performed earlier, for the passengers on the Steamer Ship *Nevada* but Martin would never miss the Tahoe's evening cruise. As the *S.S. Tahoe* rounded the point, Martin slowly got to his feet.

The last hour of sun was shining and ladies with parasols and large feather plumed hats were visible. The gentleman on board wore a variety of cloth caps, derbies, and boaters. The voice of Captain Ernest J. Pomin was heard through the ship's loud-haler as the steamer neared the Homewood Pier. "Ladies and gentlemen please observe the deckhand at the bow of the boat." People would then turn to see the bowman on the deck, holding what appeared to be a dinner plate. "As you see, the deckhand is holding a plate from the ship's galley, which he will now purposely throw over the side." Right on cue, the deckhand tossed the plate into the water. As always, the majority of people were pleasurably enthralled as to what was happening. "Ladies and gentlemen, please watch carefully as the plate sinks some fifty feet to the bottom." The throng would strain their eyes to see the plate gently sink deeper and deeper.

"Now, ladies and gentleman please observe the solitary figure at the end of Homewood Pier." As people turned to view his rotund figure, Martin, dressed in his one-piece bathing suit, would throw his arms above his head and, as majestically as he could, dive into the water.

It was a tried and tested piece of circus that captivated all who witnessed it. Martin would be beneath the surface for what seemed like an eternity. "Ladies and gentleman, those of you on the forward deck, please give the deckhand a little bit of room." A space was cleared at the bow of the steamer. A few moments later, miraculously, the discarded dinner plate would fly through the air and be brilliantly caught by the deckhand. Sometimes the deckhand might drop the plate, or miss it altogether, but never did the plate fail to reappear. "Ladies and gentleman, please observe our hero Martin Lowe back on the pier." As the steamer pulled up to the pier, Martin would be there to greet the passengers, grinning from ear to ear! In less than five minutes, since Martin had first entered the water, the plate had been retrieved and thrown back and Martin had returned to the spot where he had first started, as if by magic.

It had taken a few weeks for the trick to be perfected. Originally, Martin used to swim to the steamer with the retrieved plate and pass it up, while still in the water. But he and the captain both felt it lacked the necessary drama. They had also tried Martin starting on board the steamer, but getting up to Tahoe City was always time consuming, and diving off the side of the steamer was a little awkward and ungainly. Captain Pomin asked Martin if he could possibly dive off the pier while the steamer was on its final approach to Homewood. Martin was certain he could, and also get back onto the pier, if he could somehow throw the plate back on board instead of having to pass it up to the deckhand. Throwing the plate from the water needed practice, and it was hours before Martin got it right. Once everyone was well rehearsed and the timing was worked out just right, the trick never failed to amuse the passengers, and the visitors would recount it to their friends and family for days and weeks afterwards.

News of an earthquake survivor, who had become an aquatic showman up at Lake Tahoe, filtered down to San Francisco. So the San Francisco Examiner sent up a reporter by the name of Charles Tenwell to write a human-interest story, around the man and the star attraction he had become. Charles Tenwell went on the Steamer *Tahoe* and witnessed firsthand the amazing recovery of the plate. At first his attention, like the other passengers, was diverted from watching the water to clearing a space for the deckhand. So, he didn't see how Martin made it back on the pier in so little time.

Tenwell came to the conclusion that it wasn't humanly possible; that there had to be a piece of trickery. Was the distant figure he first saw dive from the pier, the same person who reappeared on the pier, or were there in fact two people? Charles Tenwell thought it a better story to expose the trick than to write an account of Martin's remarkable performance. So, he went on the *Tahoe* a few more times. He had to confess he was astounded each time he saw the performance. He even saw the whole performance from the Homewood pier, to be sure that it was Martin who started on the pier. He was convinced that there had to be more than one plate that perhaps several plates were already in the water. In the light of professional interest, he felt the trick had to be exposed.

Not wishing to destroy either Martin's or Captain Pomin's reputation, he decided to meet with "The Walrus" and the master of the *Tahoe*. They were both amazed that Tenwell thought it was a piece of trickery, but Tenwell was not convinced by their denials. He was determined to prove that the show, although good, was not quite as amazing as it appeared.

He smuggled his own plate on board the *Tahoe*. The plate that Tenwell brought on board was a little smaller than the *Tahoe's* dinner plate, and it was not white but a dark blue. Knowing the performance was timed to the minute, he decided to tell Pomin in advance that he wanted to substitute his own plate. Pomin at first objected, knowing that Martin would be totally ignorant of the switch. Pomin also pointed out because his plate was blue it could be a lot more difficult for Martin to find. In the end Captain Pomin acquiesced, but told Tenwell that even if Martin did not find the plate that it really proved nothing.

The captain thought it best for the passengers not to be completely disappointed. So he asked Tenwell if he minded if his plate, and a *Tahoe* dinner plate, might be used on this unique occasion. Tenwell had no objection to this, so the Captain informed the deckhand that today two plates would be used. Pomin asked the deckhand to give Martin as much of a head's up as possible, by holding both plates up high before throwing them into the water.

Martin knew something was up when he watched the deckhand hoist two plates way above his head. The sun reflected off both plates, and Martin could not easily distinguish the difference between them. It was going to be a real test to find both plates in the short amount of time. He watched the deckhand throw both plates overboard and heard the captain make his introduction. As usual, Martin raised his arms high above his head and dived into the water. Tenwell, on board with the other passengers, watched Martin disappear beneath surface, the sunlight dancing on the ripples where he had entered the water. Suddenly, Martin reappeared off the starboard side and threw a white dinner plate, which was caught by the deckhand.

The usual applause was somewhat subdued as it became apparent the blue plate was not thrown back. Captain Pomin was disappointed but still gave his usual proclamation when Martin reappeared on the pier. Tenwell was caught between disappointment and elation, but he was also aware of being ashamed that perhaps his plate had been an unfair addition. Perhaps he had not proved the trick was false anyway.

As the steamer pulled up to the pier, there was Martin with his usual grinning face, showing no sign of failure. Captain Pomin came out on the bridge and looked hard at Martin, but he just stood there smiling. The captain then looked down at Tenwell on the deck; Tenwell met the captain's eyes with a bewildered look of his own.

However, there was something about Martin's demeanor that made the captain unsure of what had gone wrong. Captain Pomin then did something he was not quite convinced he ought to do. He got back on the loud hailer and directly asked Martin what had happened to the blue plate. All eyes went to Martin on the pier, and slowly the aquatic marvel took his hands from behind his back, and to everyone's amazement and to instant cheers, in his hand was the blue plate. A cry of "That's my boy!" came from the bridge as the usually non emotional Captain, laughed and clapped his hands.

A few weeks later, in *The San Franciscan Examiner*, an article described how the beauty of Lake Tahoe offered so much to the visiting tourist and how its beauty had been enhanced, by a unique and rather curious attraction. The article was entitled "The Unbelievable Dolphin Man of Lake Tahoe!"

 *(10) Mutiny at the Inn, 1937*

The 1934 Bentley pulled up to the Glenbrook Inn, and out stepped a diminutive man. He was well dressed, as was his lady companion. They had stopped for lunch on a day tour around Lake Tahoe. It was a clear, sunny August day in 1937. Finding their way to the Inn's restaurant, they were directed to a window table with a view of the lake. The hostess who seated them did not recognize either the lady or the man.

To the hostess's surprise, the temporary waiter, who was a tall man with large ears, asked if he might be allowed to wait on the couple by the window. The hostess was only too pleased to let the waiter do this. The waiter was actually a guest in the hotel, but he insisted on helping out if and when the restaurant was busy. This particular lunchtime, half of the restaurant's twenty tables were occupied with hotel guests and visitors. It was the wish of everyone to be served by the relief waiter. Still, the couple who had arrived in the Bentley had not noticed him until he came to their table.

"The establishment reserves the right to refuse to serve anyone, especially tramps," remarked the waiter. "However, since the owner is away, we will not ask you to leave this time."

The diminutive man rose to his feet and stood as tall as he could, but the waiter was still several inches taller.

The smaller man replied, "You may refuse to serve me, but I have to say this establishment has very poor taste, especially when it comes to employing staff." Jane, the hostess, looked on in disbelief. The tension was tangible. But a small smile was evident on the waiter's face. Jane looked on as the tall waiter clumsily dropped his napkin. As the waiter bent over to pick it up, the diminutive man, unable to resist, planted his shoe on the waiter's rear and pushed him to the floor.

The flustered hostess rushed to help the waiter to his feet. She turned to the stranger and said "Do you know who your waiter is?" The diminutive man shrugged and smiled.

The waiter rolled over onto his side and smiled a broad smile. "I think he knows only too well who his waiter is, hence the lack of respect." Jane looked very confused.

The waiter got to his feet and told Jane that everything was all right. The two men squared up to each other, smiled, and gave each other a hug. The waiter then hugged the lady and sat down in a vacant seat. "What are you doing here?" asked the waiter.

"Well, I have not been here since the Gold Rush, and Paulette has never been here before."

The waiter grinned. "Well, I knew you have been around a very long time, but the Gold Rush, that would have been about ninety years ago, right?"

The small man acknowledged his friend's effort at humor. "Well, that might have been your Gold Rush but mine was less than a dozen years ago. But what of you? Are you trying to supplement your income by waiting tables?"

"I am thinking of getting divorced. Or rather, I am here to get my Nevadan state residency, so I can get divorced. Anyway, I like to wait tables. It's therapeutic to the soul to serve one's fellow man!"

The waiter told Jane that since the restaurant was not too busy, he was going to join his friends. The friends ate, drank, and laughed the day away; the couple's planned tour of the lake was shelved. The waiter suggested the couple stay through the evening and spend the night at the Inn as his guests.

Later that evening,

Jane learned the identity of the small man and his partner, and now felt she would never live it down. The restaurant was busier than usual that evening, since word had gotten out among the locals that there was a trick to be played on certain unsuspecting customers.

Paulette was sitting at a table by herself. When the chosen couple came in, they were purposely led to the table adjacent to hers. One of the waitresses came over and gave them time to look over the menu. After looking at the menu, the gentleman ordered the trout, the lady ordered the pork loin, and they ordered some wine. When the food came out, Paulette leaned over from her table and inquired what they had ordered. Upon being told, Paulette told the man that she, too, had eaten the trout, but it was somewhat dry. At this time, the tall waiter came by and filled up the couple's wine glasses. Paulette spoke directly to the waiter, "This gentleman has ordered the trout and it is a little dry."

The waiter told the couple that he would pass on their comments to the chef. "Well, I wasn't exactly complaining," said the startled gentleman, who looked hard and long at the waiter. "Aren't you - ?" The waiter cut him off and left for the kitchen. He returned and told the couple the chef would be right out.

The couple started whispering among themselves. "I feel so embarrassed, I wasn't complaining, it was the lady who said the fish was dry, I didn't say anything." The man looked around the room. "Everyone is looking at us." The lady looked around and, yes, everyone was indeed looking at them. "I don't know what just happened. I don't want a scene with chef!" the man said, in an anguished voice.

"Just tell the waiter that you have no complaint dear." The lady patted the back of her partner's hand reassuringly.

Then the man commented. "That waiter looks exactly like that film star. But it couldn't be. What would he be doing serving table at a restaurant?"

Suddenly, the lights in the restaurant went out, and in dramatic fashion the doors leading to the kitchen swung open. Silhouetted by the bright lights of the kitchen behind, stood the darkened outline of the chef. It was such a piece of grand drama that all movement in the restaurant stopped. The lights of the restaurant went back on. The chef wore a chef's hat and carried a rolling pin which he banged into his open palm several times. Every time he banged the rolling pin small puffs of flour filled the air. He stood there for a minute or two and then shuffled into the restaurant with his feet almost at right angles.

The chef was small and had an unmistakable moustache. Everyone, patrons, and staff alike, looked at the chef as he penguined his way into the room. Still smacking the rolling pin into his open hand, the look of determination on his face suggested he was ready do battle with anyone who dared to complain. The chef first spoke to the tall waiter. The waiter gestured toward the couple. The chef glared in their direction. The conversation with the waiter continued and grew ever more heated. It was obvious that the chef was becoming angry. The argument between the chef and waiter ended with the waiter being unceremoniously kicked in the behind. The couple was so taken aback that they dared not speak.

Paulette got up and spoke to the chef. She told him that the trout served to the gentlemen was dry. The chef whirled around and faced the man. He tipped his hat to the lady, stared at the gentleman and smacked the pin against his open hand again. After a few more smacks with the rolling pin, the chef put it down, rolled up his sleeves, took an empty seat from Paulette's table, and sat in between the couple. He grabbed a fork, took the gentleman's meal and proceeded to eat it. He looked up at the lady, smiled a pursed-lip smile, and tipped his hat. Between every mouthful, he would stare at the gentleman, twitch his moustache, turn to the lady, tip his hat, and smile again. Without a word the chef ate the whole meal, finally putting his finger tips to his lips he blew a kiss. The waiter came across and said, "Well, obviously the chef thinks the trout is very good!" Neither the gentleman nor the lady had spoken: the man's mouth was wide open, and the lady's eyes were wider than saucers. The waiter spoke again "Would you perhaps like the chef to prepare, or perhaps (the waiter paused for effect) EAT, something else for you? Howls of laughter rang around the dining room.

To the couple's amazement, the chef got up from his seat to thunderous applause, which he acknowledged by bowing to all parts of the dining room. The chef then outstretched his hand to the waiter, who in turned bowed to further applause. The waiter then turned to Paulette, who also received a round of applause. The couple was totally nonplussed. The grinning waiter came over to the couple and told them that he was indeed who they had thought he might be, and that they had literally shared their meal with the foremost comic actor in the world.

At the realization that they were the brunt of a bizarre joke, the couple was red faced but also delighted to have been a part of the night's entertainment. Many people came by to congratulate them on being such good sports. The Inn gave them a complimentary meal, and they gratefully shared a drink with their tormentors.

The Players

The Waiter...Clark Gable

The Lady-friend.............................Paulette Goddard

The Chef..Charlie Chaplin

(11) In the Halls
of Zeus (The Bid) 1955

Alex Cushing stood six feet four inches tall and was a walking contradiction of man. It was said he could sell sandals to an Eskimo but he could not make small talk with a neighbor. However, the greatest coup he ever pulled off was to promote an enclosed meadow, in a remote part of the Sierra Nevada in California, as a possible site for the preeminent winter sports event in the world.

It is the last week of 1954 where we start the story of the most outrageous, totally implausible, highly improbable choosing of Squaw Valley to host the1960 Winter Olympics.

+   +   +   +

It was the day after Christmas. The tall man was seated inside the fifty-room Squaw Valley Lodge reading the San Francisco Chronicle. A headline made him sit up. Anchorage, Alaska, and Reno, Nevada, had both submitted bids to host the Winter Olympics in 1960. The bids had joined bids from Sun Valley, Idaho; Lake Placid, New York; and a joint bid from Aspen and Colorado Springs. The United States Olympic Committee was supposed to have made their selection back in November. Detroit had already been chosen for America's entry for the 1960 Summer Olympics, but the choice of entry for the winter candidate had been deferred due to the late entries from both Anchorage and Reno.

Alex looked out the window to see people using one of the two tow ropes on his intimate and friendly little Squaw Valley ski area, the place he had called home for the past five years. Wayne Poulsen, the original pioneer of developing Squaw, had been looking for financial backers. Alex, a Wall Street lawyer with connections in New York, had joined Poulsen in forming the Squaw Valley Development Corporation, in 1949. Alex looked back at the headline. He puzzled over the mention of Reno, Nevada. Where would Reno hold Olympic downhill events? Slide Mountain, on the eastern range of the Sierras, some thirty miles away to Reno's southwest, was the probable answer. Maybe Alex could offer Squaw as a viable alternative to Slide Mountain. Then again, Reno would probably not want to have the skiing events in a California location. The more he thought about it, the more he thought. Why join Reno at all? Perhaps with some imagination and investment, Squaw could hold every event itself, within walking distance. How much of an advantage would that be? Putting forward the name of Squaw Valley, would be worth the publicity alone.

He read the Olympic decree: "The honor of the Olympics is always awarded to a city, never to a country!" He worried that Squaw Valley would not even qualify as a village, let alone a city. Undeterred, he made up his mind to phone the USOC in the morning.

"Hello, is that the offices of the United States Olympic Committee?" Alex was pretty sure it was, because he had tried every other number imaginable.

The voice on the other end belonged to a pleasant lady. "Yes it is. Can I help you?"

"Well, I am a bit new to this, but I am wondering: is it still possible to put forward a place for the site of the Winter Olympics?"

The lady was still extremely polite, "A place, sir? What do you mean?"

"Well, I have, or rather we have, a ski area in the mountains of California, and we were hoping we might submit it as a possible site to host the Olympics. But I don't know the actual requirements needed."

The lady laughed a little. "Requirements, sir? Well, I think the only requirement is that the location has to be in America."

Alex laughed, too. "That's wonderful, because California is in America!"

The lady chuckled again. "Well, you are quite fortunate, the choice for the American site for the Winter Games should have been put forward to the International Olympic Committee already. But the decision has been postponed until the New Year. The IOC is due to meet in Paris in June, so the USOC has to make its selection in about two weeks."

Alex was pleased, but realized he would have to move fast. "Well, what should I do next?"

"Well, submit your plans in writing to the committee as quickly as possible and that's about it!" The lady gave the necessary address and she told Alex that the committee would meet on January 7.

Alex wrote and rewrote all the pros that Squaw Valley had in its favor. The disadvantage that Reno had, in being thirty miles from the nearest mountain, was less of a problem than he had first thought. Oslo had, during their hosted Games in1952, held their ski events some seventy miles outside of the city. Still, Alex felt it was an advantage for Squaw that it was largely undeveloped and that it would have ample room for purpose- built arenas; maybe a new housing complex for the athletes, within a comfortable distance. "Boy, that's a big advantage!" Alex thought to himself. It had been twenty-three years since the US had hosted the Games. All the other Winter Olympics, beside Lake Placid in1932, had been held in Europe. Added to this, was the undeniable truth that the US had a better economy than post-war Europe.

Having dashed off all the benefits, he then listed all the possible disadvantages. To his chagrin, the same item appeared on both lists: the fact that Squaw was largely undeveloped. The fact that there was no paved road into Squaw Valley was another disadvantage. The fact that no one outside California and the immediate area knew of Squaw Valley was another one.

Alex chatted at length with his Ski School Director, Jo Marrilac. Marrilac was initially taken aback, but after some thought, the Frenchman gave his whole-hearted support and affirmation that Squaw could indeed be transformed into a world-class ski area.

Alex drove down to San Francisco to see whether he could gain the support of the city newspapers. His first stop was at the *San Francisco Chronicle*. The managing editor made it more or less clear that they would support Reno's bid, due to the amount of advertising revenue the Nevada city brought in for the paper. A little deflated, Alex moved on to the *San Francisco Examiner.* Charles Meyer, the Examiner's editor, was grinning when Alex told him of the reception he had received at the Chronicle.

"Well, we are a little more pro-California here at the Examiner. We'll be glad to support you!" Meyer got on the phone and asked Curley Grieve, the sports editor, to join them.

Once Grieve came in, Meyer said to Alex, "So tell us what your aspirations are and how realistic they might be."

Alex, buoyed by Meyer's enthusiasm, went through all the advantages he had conceived the night before, without mentioning any of the disadvantages. To Alex's further delight, Curley Grieve made copious notes.

The next day, a reporter ran into the editor's office at the Chronicle and thrust a copy of the Examiner under Thieriot's nose. The editor snorted as he read the headline: "Squaw Valley Enters Bid for 1960 Games, with Backing of Local Community!"

Thieriot looked up at his reporter, "It's a publicity stunt that I didn't think was worthy of our paper, and besides, Charlie Meyer is just trying to goad me! It will come to nothing, and Mister Cushing will be yesterday's news come the New Year. But let Charlie have his little bit of fun for a couple of weeks!"

Having spent the night in San Francisco, Alex drove back to Squaw Valley, via Sacramento, and visited Clint Mosher, the Examiner's political correspondent. Alex introduced himself, but Mosher had already read the morning copy of the Examiner. "Yes, you are causing a bit of stir already, Mister Cushing. You've got Biz Johnson dying to meet you!"

Alex was a little bemused. "Who is Biz Johnson?"

"You don't know your local senator from Placer County, the Right Honorable Harold 'Biz' Johnson?"

"Sadly, no, I don't. But I would be glad of an introduction!"

"I think we had better go and see him straightaway and put you both out of your misery." Mosher made a quick phone call, and he and Alex went off to the state capital building.

Alex was first greeted by an exuberant Biz Johnson and then by several other senators. One senator couldn't contain his enthusiasm. "I've actually skied Squaw Valley!"

Johnson told Alex to wait in his office while he went and saw Governor Goodwin Knight.

When Johnson walked back into his office, he was beaming. "Alex, the governor has been given the go-ahead to reintroduce a bill that was first used to get the Olympic Games to Los Angeles, in 1932."

Alex was delighted. "What does that mean?" he inquired.

"It means, if passed, a grant of one million dollars!"

Alex sat down on the senator's leather sofa. One million dollars for the one million thoughts that were racing through his head!

Alex had originally not thought of going to New York to talk to the USOC, but he was told in no uncertain terms that he had to go. New York was his old stomping ground, and he thought he might use the occasion to catch up with a few old acquaintances. He arrived at Idlewild Airport on the evening of January 6 and took a cab to his Manhattan hotel. He contacted two of his friends Laurence Rockefeller and sports editor Bob Cooke at the Herald Tribune.

Laurence told Alex he could use Radio City Music Hall to show his film "Squaw Valley Winter." Bob told Alex he would write a supporting piece in the Tribune.

Alex had not been back to San Francisco or Sacramento since his visit ten days earlier. However, when Alex met Lyman Bingman, United States Olympic Committee representative, at the Manhattan Biltmore Hotel on the morning of January 7, he was surprised to discover that USOC had received calls from nearly everyone at the California Legislature as well as several calls from the Examiner. "I guess you got the whole state behind you, Mister Cushing!"

"Yes, it seems a spark of an idea that has ignited a few imaginations!"

"I understand you know the Rockefellers, too?"

As way of an apology, Alex told Bingham that he was in fact originally from New York and that Laurence Rockefeller was himself an investor in Squaw Valley. "Would it be possible to show my Squaw Valley film to the committee as part of my presentation?"

"Only if you provide the popcorn, too!" joked Bingman. "Now, would you like to come in and meet the rest of the committee?"

The committee was astounded that Alex was a one-man show. He started very deliberately but was immediately peppered with questions. He had planned a solemn presentation, but he reveled in answering all the questions. The questions were on climate, snow conditions, ease of access, accommodations, financing, existing facilities, proposed development, culinary services, being able to cater to a wide variety of different nationalities, transportation, length of journey from Reno, security, ticket sales, events, and entertainment. Alex enjoyed himself, as all his answers seem to satisfy the committee. At last, Mr. Bingham addressed the other members of the committee.

"Mister Cushing had intended to present a film, but I think all our questions have been answered, so I don't think it necessary now."

With that, Alex walked out of the room, leaving the committee to deliberate.

He met some of the Reno delegates outside waiting to give their presentation. Apparently, the committee had already seen the representatives of Sun Valley, Lake Placid, Anchorage, and Aspen/Colorado Springs.

Alex went back to his hotel, where his friend Laurence Rockefeller had been geared up to take the committee to Radio City.

Alex met his friend's questioning stare. "It's not necessary, Laurence."

Laurence looked a little disappointed. "Why, are they not interested?"

Alex explained over lunch all that had occurred and how he'd hardly had time to think. "I've got to call later and hear whatever choice they've made. I feel I did my best, and I can't second-guess anything now. It's all in the hands of the Olympic Gods!"

"Well, let's have a deserved drink in the bar. I want to be here when you get the news!"

After sharing a couple of drinks, Alex got up and told his friend he would use the public phone in the lobby.

Alex closed the door to the telephone booth behind him and dialed the number of the Biltmore Hotel. An operator put him through to the USOC meeting room. "Mister Bingham, is that you? It's Alex Cushing from Squaw Valley."

"Yes, Mister Cushing, well we have given Squaw Valley due consideration......."

Alex's heart was in his mouth ".....and we have decided to select Squaw Valley's name to go forward to the International Committee next June as America's choice for the site of the Winter Games of 1960. Congratulations!"

"Alex responded professionally. He thanked Mr. Bingham and asked him to thank the other members of the committee.

Once off the phone, Alex's head starting swimming. Perhaps he was a little drunk. The reality of what had just happened was not even a dream two weeks ago. He chuckled to himself and tried to appear stoic, but for the first time since arriving in New York, he allowed his friend to see some emotion! His friend applauded in response to Alex's huge grin.

"I knew you'd do it! All those years of being a lawyer haven't gone to waste!"

Alex shook his head. "I am afraid I never had your confidence, and I still can't believe this is happening! This was just to create some good publicity."

"Alex, be serious for a moment. This isn't just your dream anymore. This dream belongs to quite few others now! Anyway, it's no longer a dream, it is a hope, and it deserves your all! You've got a good part of California behind you. Now get the whole country behind you!"

After New York, Alex went to visit Avery Brundage in Chicago. Brundage had been given the presidency of the International Olympic Committee in 1952. An American in that position seemed like a godsend, but Brundage was not so delighted by the USOC's choice. "They must have taken leave of their senses. On paper, there is no chance of Squaw Valley being selected by the IOC. All I suggest to you, Mister Cushing, is not to waste the five months between now and Paris. You will be appearing before the European aristocracy, and no amount of American charm will win them over. Unless you can convince them you can turn your picnic area into a world-class resort!"

Back at Squaw, Alex told his friend Jo Marrilac, "I don't think Avery Brundage is on our side." Marshall Hazeltine, another of Alex's friends from Harvard, was an able linguist, and, having once worked for the US State Department, Alex knew he could be helpful in approaching foreign IOC members. Perhaps with Marrilac and Hazeltine, Alex could put a little less American brashness to their bid and make it a little more palatable to foreign dignitaries. When it came to going before the International Committee, Alex was not going to be a one-man show.

Having taken Avery Brundage's advice, Alex decided to devote every wakening hour of the next five months to "The Bid," as it became known in the Tahoe area. Over the next six weeks, various architects and contractors were summarily invited to offer plans for the necessary amenities: an Olympic village to house a thousand athletes, an Olympic ski jump, a speed-skating circuit, an indoor skating rink, parking for twelve thousand vehicles, a bob sleigh run, etc. Even the minimal requirements would send the cost skyrocketing. The California legislature's offer of one million dollars was not going to be enough!

Eventually, blueprints were made and artists' impressions were drawn. "It's no use," Alex sighed "We don't have anything of substance to show the IOC. How can we convince the IOC, that we are capable of staging the Olympics by showing them drawings? They won't want to wade through stacks of blueprints. Let's remember, we are competing with established ski resorts that practically need little or no development."

"How about photographs, of the valley, as it is now, with superimposed negatives of how it will look like once the arenas are built?" Hazeltine suggested.

"You would need to take photographs looking down on the mountain, as well as the meadow," countered Marrilac.

Alex looked thoughtful. "Well, we could hire a plane."

"What about a model?" offered Hazeltine.

"A model of what, exactly?" Alex wanted more from his Harvard classmate.

"We build a three-dimensional model of the entire mountain. The meadow, with all the new structures in place, the Olympic village, the skating arena, the downhill course, the bob sleigh run, and the ski jump! We take photographs of the model and show the committee."

Hazeltine looked over to Marrilac, who was nodding his approval.

"Who could build and design such a model?" was the question Cushing left hanging in the air.

Architect Rudolph G. Theurkauf's scale model of San Francisco was considered a work of genius when it went on exhibit at the 1933 World's Fair in Chicago. The model of San Francisco was thirty feet long by fifteen feet wide and featured forty thousand miniature buildings. It was considered the greatest model city ever built.

As a resident of Sausalito, Theurkauf already knew that Squaw Valley was vying for the Olympics. A model designed by Theurkauf would have been cost-prohibitive under normal circumstances. However, being a loyal Californian, a price of three thousand dollars was negotiated with the Sausalito architect. Artistic impressions of the sports facilities for the Olympics had already been drawn, so it was Theurkauf's job to translate those ideas into depth and dimension. He suggested a model of Squaw at one-sixteenth to scale, which meant the model would be twelve feet by six feet.

The topographical model was made of plaster of Paris, and it took several workers six weeks to finish. The finished article was praised and admired by everyone who saw it, and it alone made believers of even the most ardent naysayers.

It was near to Easter that Alex decided to go to Europe and appeal directly to some of the member countries. Every member country of the IOC had one vote and the majority of votes would determine who would be awarded the Games. While in Europe, Alex realized how stiff the competition would be. Garmisch and St. Moritz were world-renowned ski areas, but it seemed from everybody that Alex came in contact with that Innsbruck was the overwhelming favorite. Unlike the other two, Innsbruck and Austria had never hosted the Games and everyone was sure their turn had come.

On a visit to St Moritz, Alex ran into George Weller. Weller had been a well-known war correspondent and Pulitzer Prize winner in 1943. He was the first American reporter to visit Nagasaki a month after the city was leveled by the second atom bomb in August 1945. Now, ten years later, George Weller was the Paris bureau chief for the *Chicago Daily News*.

Weller and Cushing met in the bar of their St. Moritz hotel. They had both been at Harvard, but Weller was Cushing's senior by four years. They exchanged niceties and stories of Harvard. In their conversation, it came to light that Alex was headed up to Garmisch and, by coincidence so was Weller. Alex offered George a ride in his car, and the two enjoyed each other's company. On the drive up, Alex told

Weller of his mission to drum up support for his Olympic bid. In Garmisch, the two Harvard men went their separate ways. After Garmisch, Alex drove down to Innsbruck and on to Cortina. Cortina d'Ampezzo, Italy, had been awarded the Winter Games of 1956, and it was natural that Alex should check in to see how Cortina was fairing with their preparations. While in Cortina, Alex ran into George Weller a second time. In fact, they were again staying at the same hotel.

George Weller joined Alex for breakfast and asked how his quest was going.

"Well, it's been a bit of a mixed bag. Everyone is very agreeable, but no real commitments as yet. I am going to see the Cortina delegation today. Everyone seems certain Innsbruck will be awarded the Games. I don't think they are taking me too seriously! I have agreed to leave the French to my native Frenchman Marrilac."

"Marrilac? Jo Marrilac of the French Resistance?" asked Weller.

"Yes, he is my ski school instructor!"

"Your ski school instructor at Squaw is Jo Marrilac? At Squaw Valley. In California?" There was a tone of disbelief in Weller's voice.

Alex laughed. "Yes, and he is convinced Squaw would make a great Olympic venue!"

"Well, why isn't he here with you now? How can you leave such ace in the hole, in the hole?"

"Well, it's our last big ski weekend of the season. I cannot spare him now. But I'll have Jo come with me to Paris in June."

"Alex, take my advice: get Marrilac out here as soon as you can. Some of the Europeans are still a little stuffy, and Marrilac will give the whole bid a respectability we couldn't hope to match."

"*We* couldn't match? What do you mean 'we'?"

Weller smiled. "Look, Alex, you can't possibly be taken seriously as a one-man show. Do you mind if I come with you today? There may be at least a story in this, and maybe I could be of some assistance as well."

Alex's face broke into a big smile. "I would be honored to have your company!"

Alex felt the Italians were much more receptive than either the Swiss and Germans had been. After Italy, Alex went home to America, via London. In London, Alex looked up some acquaintances of his friend Marshall Hazeltine. The question the Brits most wanted to know was whether Ike was fully behind the Squaw bid. Alex enthusiastically said yes, but the truth was, besides signing an appropriation bill for some federal financing, Alex did not know the president's personal feelings. Alex left London knowing the Brits would back any bid supported by Eisenhower. Back in the States, Hazeltine reassured Alex that the president and the country were totally committed to the bid. It was now time to persuade the world, particularly those outside Europe.

With the help of Marrilac and Hazeltine, an in-depth argument for Squaw was written in English, Spanish, and French. It was further agreed that Alex would return to Europe with Marrilac, Hazeltine, and Weller, well before the IOC meeting in June. IOC members were contacted outside Europe and offers made to pay for members to fly to Paris in time for the vote. A large proportion of the Latin America countries declared their support for Squaw Valley. With the Brits seemingly on board, it was possible that Australia and New Zealand would follow suit. Certainly, the Canadians were favorable. Still, Squaw would need support from enough European countries to win the bid. Marrilac's appearance would be crucial. The French would be persuaded by him, and maybe some of the Scandinavian countries might be won over, too.

Cushing's tack to declare that the Olympics belong to the world and not just Europe certainly struck a chord with those outside Europe. However, there was a lot of empathy inside Europe for the Austrians. Austrian skiers were always among the best in the world, and there was a determined feeling that the Austrians were overdue to host the Games. In Europe, it was inconceivable that Innsbruck would lose to the likes of Squaw Valley. Even the British felt their support of Squaw Valley was a token of their friendship for America; they really did not see Innsbruck losing the bid.

It was too finely balanced. Alex was already banking on Marrilac persuading the French and hoping that the Belgians or the Dutch might support the American cause following the liberation of Europe ten years earlier. Alex needed every advantage to squeeze the three or four votes that were unaccounted for. It was decided that Weller would go to South Africa before Europe.

Alex and Marrilac went back to Europe in late May. Marrilac was, as expected, greeted as a hero by the French, and his affirmation that Squaw was indeed capable of hosting the games was enough to win the support of the Federation of International Skiing.

The Germans were less enthusiastic and they asked Marrilac to compare Squaw Valley to any European ski resort. To their amazement, and ironically, he compared Squaw favorably to Austria's best loved-ski area Kitzbuhel. The Germans eyed Marrilac suspiciously, but the Frenchman again showed his determined resistance and assured everyone within hearing that he spoke the truth. Still, Cushing felt his photographs of Theurkauf's model did not do enough to show the whole hill and the facilities in relation to each other. Frustratingly, the photographs still needed explanation, and Alex rued not having the model so the IOC could see it personally.

Marshall Hazeltine joined Cushing and Marrilac in Paris in early June. Although there had been progress, it was certain that a better impression had to be made.

Alex turned to his friends and said, "If Mohammed won't come to the mountain, we will bring the mountain to Mohammed. We have to have the model here in Paris for all delegates to see before the vote."

"How is that possible? It must weigh a ton!" Marshall Hazeltine, looked at his friend Alex quizzically.

"Closer to one and a half tons. Sheer lunacy, I know. But we need every advantage, and I think it will improve our chances immeasurably."

A cargo plane was hurriedly chartered to fly from Reno to Paris, and on board was the three-thousand-pound model. A delighted Alex met the plane at Le Bourget airport, with a rented truck to take the model to the Sorbonne University, where the IOC was due to meet. Sadly, despite several attempts, it was impossible to get the model inside the building. George Weller, who had come back to Paris to help in the final stretch, was able to persuade the American Ambassador to come to the rescue. The model was taken to the American Embassy and put on display inside the embassy entry hall. Fortunately, it was only a short walk to the American Embassy from the Sorbonne.

On the afternoon of June 15, 1955, the IOC awarded the 1960 Summer Games to Rome, beating out Detroit, Mexico City and Tokyo in the process. The choice of Rome, just might have been a game changer, it probably won a few uncommitted votes over to the Squaw Valley, because Squaw was the only non-European bid for the Winter Games.

On the morning of June 17, Alex went for an early morning walk along the river Seine. It was a glorious sunny morning. On his way back to the hotel, he stopped at a typical Parisian café for coffee and freshly baked croissants. He sat at one of the tables outside on the sidewalk. The café was on a densely tree-lined boulevard with a glimpse of the Eiffel Tower. After his coffee, he lazily walked back to the hotel. He wanted to experience the joy of this beautiful morning feeling a little longer, before he rolled up his sleeves for the final battle. Paris in all its glory made him feel good. All his lieutenants would be there with him, and the model was ready for viewing at the embassy. What had started as a flight of fantasy, for some extra publicity, had grown to within a hairbreadth of reality.

"It's going to be Innsbruck!" They were the first words that greeted the three Americans and one Frenchman, as they walked into one of the many buildings of Paris's best known and oldest university. It was the voice of German pessimism that Alex had heard for months now. "How can it not be Innsbruck?" the voice questioned.

Alex made a bee line for Avery Brundage and asked the IOC president if he might be permitted to take the voting delegates over to the American Embassy to view the model of Squaw Valley.

"Well, I guess I would not be welcomed back home if I ruled against it. Only the French delegates are not here yet, but I understand Mister Marrilac has already convinced them to support you. So I guess now would be as good a time as any!"

Everyone, including the IOC president followed Alex and his three partners, over to the embassy. Alex used the fifteen-minute walk to introduce himself to some of the delegates that he had yet to meet and to give a little boost to his presentation. At the embassy, the delegates encouragingly lingered over the model for longer than expected. Alex assured the members of the IOC that the model was an exact replica of the valley. The Squaw Valley quartet smiled at each other as murmurs of approval were audible from many of the delegates. Their concentration was interrupted by a sudden commotion at the door. It was the excited French delegates bursting into the embassy. Looking at the model, the Frenchmen went up to Marrilac and started planting congratulatory slaps on the back of their beloved compatriot. "Mon Dieu!" "C'est Manifique!" Their late arrival could not have been better had it been planned.

Not long after all the delegates had returned to the Sorbonne, and the first round of voting took place. There was no clear winner, so it was decided that the third and fourth place names - Garmisch and St. Moritz would be withdrawn and all delegates would choose between either, Innsbruck or Squaw Valley. It was an agonizing wait for everyone concerned. Alex looked at Hazeltine, Weller, and Marillac. He knew he had left nothing to chance and there was nothing left to do. Graciously, he walked over to the Innsbruck delegation and offered his hand and good wishes. Marrilac watched Alex shake hands with the Austrians, and he walked over and shook their hands, too!

Inside the IOC meeting room, the votes were being counted and Avery Brundage was getting really nervous. It looked like it might be a 31-31 tie and he would have to cast the deciding vote. It was the worst scenario he could possibly imagine. If he voted for Squaw he would be accused of favoritism. If he voted for Innsbruck he would be accused of betrayal. This was the worst moment of his presidency and for once he did not know what he would do. There was a recount, and after confirmation it was evident that Brundage's deciding vote would not be necessary. The final vote was thirty votes for Innsbruck and thirty-two for Squaw! In less than six months, a casual whim by an individual had produced an extraordinary result for the ski business of Tahoe.

Alex made a trans-Atlantic phone call via the international operator..., after a few rings a voice came on the line.

"Hello."

"Who's that?" Alex asked

"It's Chad," the voice innocently declared.

"Is this the Squaw Valley Lodge?

"Yes, it is, but I don't work here. I am just minding the desk while Rachel's gone to collect the mail."

"Chad, this is Alex Cushing from Paris, tell Rachel, to tell everyone our bid for the Olympics has been approved by the IOC."

"Oh, is that good? Sorry, what is your name again?"

"It's Alex Cushing, Rachel's boss, from Paris. We have just been awarded the Olympic Games in 1960."

"Well, that must be good," Chad continued.

"Yes, it is. Chad, tell Rachel I'll call her later."

 **(12) Sesquicentennial (The Tribute)**

On a snowy winter's night in 2006, the traffic was backed up on Highway 50 at a Caltrans chain control near the small community of Strawberry. Caltrans were checking vehicles to make sure that all non-four-wheel-drive cars had their chains fitted.

The traffic was backed up for nearly a mile as each car was individually inspected. It was, and still is, a common occurrence on the roads leading up to Lake Tahoe in the winter time. On this one occasion, however, many drivers waiting in the long line of vehicles were amused to see three young men dressed as pioneers slide on past them on longboards with long poles. Many car occupants honked their horns, and the three friends cheerfully waved back to the people as they slid on by. They were going to longboard across the Sierras as a 150th anniversary tribute to Snowshoe Thompson's epic travails across the Sierra Nevada of the mid 1800s.

Unlike their hero, however, the three had no mail to carry, and each had packed a sub-zero thermal insulated sleeping bag. They also had the benefit of Highway 50, which they intended to use for the journey up to Sierra Ski Ranch before heading off into the wilderness. They expected to travel all night and camp after the sun had risen. They had flashlights, another thing their hero would have been without. There were no grizzlies or wolves as in Thompson's day, but they felt it wise to be safe. Very few of the dangers that faced Thompson still existed. But still this was an unknown adventure, and the young men felt inspired to take on the all that nature might throw at them. As they pushed on up Highway 50, the snow fell at a steady rate as a fairly moderate storm closed in.

1856

John A. Thompson was born in Tinn, in the Telemark region of Norway, on April 30, 1827. As a young boy he learned how to get around on the snow and ice by tying flat boards to his feet. Norwegians could skate, and schuss great distances on these flat boards. The boards were shaped from straight grained-wood, and how long they were depended on how tall the boy or man. The length was determined by how high you could reach above your head: for a four-foot boy, they might be six feet long; for a six-foot man they might be nine feet long. A pole became an essential part of the equipment for a long-boarder. It was used for balance, it was used to change direction, it was used to reduce speed, and it was used as a brake. The pole was held horizontally for balance, trailed to either side to change direction, and held in between the legs to slow or to stop.

Thompson's father died when he was just two years old. When he was ten years old, he came to America with his mother and older brother. Originally, the family settled in the Mid-west, but two years after the Gold Rush in 1849, the young Norwegian came out to California. He was six feet tall, blond haired, with stunning blue eyes, and every inch an athlete. Added to his physique was a genuine caring nature for his fellow man. After trying his hand at gold panning, Thompson chose to become a rancher and settle near Markleeville, about thirty miles south of Lake Tahoe.

While living on his new ranch, the young Norwegian answered a call from the United States Postal Service. The US Mail needed help to deliver the mail over the Sierra Nevada Mountains during the winter months. The mail would arrive by ship in San Francisco and would make its way to Sacramento, but when the heavy snows came, the mail could not be delivered to those living beyond the foothills. Before the telegraph and the Transcontinental Railroad, communities on the eastern side of the Sierras, were cut off from the rest of civilization, until the snows melted. A winter mail delivery was needed over the mountains from Hangtown (Placerville) to Mormon Station (Genoa) in the Carson Valley, a distance of ninety miles. When Thompson offered his services, and explained he intended to use wooden boards tied to his feet by leather straps, some people laughed, others were incredulous, but no one thought the Norwegian sane. When they told Thompson that some of his predecessors had never been seen again, he asserted he would be fine. Buoyed by his confidence, the US Postal Service decided to take a chance on the crazy Viking.

In was the winter of 1856 that Thompson first set off. Many of the townsfolk were there to see him go. The mail pack he was carrying weighed more than seventy-five pounds. Since the snow line was a few hundred feet above Placerville,

Thompson's long-boards were strapped to his back as he hiked out of town. The oak long-boards themselves weighed another twenty-five pounds, so the bemused townspeople watched Thompson disappear, carrying more than a hundred pounds on his back. For provisions he packed dried beef jerky, home-made biscuits, coffee, a small pot for melting snow, a small axe, matches, and his Bible. He took no gun and no blankets and as he hiked alongside the American River on his way east, many locals doubted they would see this brave young blond-haired man again.

Thompson hiked maybe eight miles before he saw enough snow to strap on his long-boards. He followed the river up until the first waterfall. He needed to travel north-eastward, so he kept the sun at his back as best as he could. In the sunshine, the snow cloyed to his boards. The snow hardened as the sun fell behind the mountains which made the going easier.

On this his first mail run, he purposely chose the nearest clear day to a full moon. Having left the American river behind, he decided to press on. He would travel up the western range until he could see the distant eastern range and the valley which separated the two. The Norwegian travelled more than forty miles, and well into the night, before he stopped. He chose to make camp by the side of a small, slanting, dead fir. He cut the lower limbs off of another fir, dug a hole in the snow, and lined it with enough branches to create a soft bed. He chopped kindling and built a fire underneath the dead tree. The improvised bed was on the opposite side to the slant of the small tree, and he lay with his feet towards the fire. He put the mail bag under his head, pulled his big hat over his eyes, and went to sleep.

He awoke maybe five hours later. The burning tree had collapsed, as he had expected, but it had fallen harmlessly into the snow. It was cold, it was dark, and the fire had largely burnt out but some of the charcoal still glowed. He placed some of his home made biscuits carefully in among the glowing embers. Melted enough snow to make a three-quarter cup of warm coffee and ate the toasted biscuits, before continuing on.

He planned to stop again in the middle of day, when the softened snow made his progress slower. His aim was to reach the top of the eastern range by the end of his second day. Having gotten to the top of the western range, the next ten to fifteen miles would be mostly downhill, and he hoped he would be in the Lake Valley area before the sun came up.

He looked down from the ridge. Going downhill would be faster but certainly a lot more dangerous. He took it cautiously through the trees. When he came to a clearing, the snow looked like a motionless sea. Everything looked blue in the light of the full moon; it was a beautiful sight, but he was not going to stop to admire it. Having struggled uphill for most of the previous day, he was now looking forward to making some rapid progress. The Norwegian swung his pole into the horizontal position and skated down the initial slope. Gravity took over and he went into the tuck position. As he picked up considerable speed, the snow covered rocks, and the snow laden trees, blurred as he flew by them.

Four days later, Jack Glenville had just finished digging his way to the trail outside his cabin. He knew nothing of the Norwegian who was delivering the mail over the Sierras. Jack had built his cabin on the Johnson's Cut-Off, halfway between the pass and Placerville. At this time of year, his cabin had snow up to its roofline. During bad storms he would have to wait until the sky cleared before he could venture outside and dig himself out.

Having dug his way from his cabin's front door, Jack was standing on the trail, when he heard a muffled cry. Slowly, he turned and looked uphill, but he could not quite make out what was in his line of vision. Suddenly, there was a louder shout, and it was coming from a gray shape that was growing ever larger by the second. Glenville realized what it was only just in time to dive out of the way. He hurriedly scrambled back to his feet to see the disappearing shape grow ever smaller as it went further down the trail. It had been a man going faster than a train, faster than any horse could run!

Five days after he had left on his outbound journey. Thompson was on his way back. The man at the local US Mail office had only spared an occasional thought for the good-looking Norwegian. Everyone in Placerville had gone about their normal business. A driver of horse-drawn buggy headed into Placerville from the east, recognized the tall blond figure hiking along the American river. The driver stopped and offered the young man a ride. Thompson thanked him but turned the offer down. The driver drove on and when he came into the center of Placerville, the driver spoke to some of the town's people gathered in the winter sunshine.

"He's back! The Norwegian is back! I just passed him twenty minutes ago! He'll be here in another half an hour or so!" The news ran around the town, and the man at the US Mail was told by one of the traders that the Norwegian had been sighted. The locals started to run to the eastern edge of town. It was something like another fifteen minutes before they saw the young Norwegian hero walking with his longboards tied to his back. He smiled at all the townsfolk as he passed them by. As on the outbound journey, he had covered the last eight miles on foot. The US Mail man was delightfully surprised as Thompson handed him the mail from Genoa.

Thompson had averaged thirty-five miles a day, up and down two mountain ranges, back and forth through unfamiliar territory, with no map, travelling mostly by night! It was acclaimed as a super human effort that was beyond the feat of even the fittest individual.

He had lost contact with his two friends. He saw them fifteen minutes earlier but lost them in the wind-driven snow. The storm had slowly abated, but it was still snowing and huge clouds still obscured the light of the moon.

He strained his eyes to see, but he feared the slope in front of him was a little too severe to risk a straight run. So he started diagonally down the steep incline, keeping his uphill knee bent. He held the pole at an angle, so while the pole's top half was in front of him the lower half trailed in the snow behind his feet. It took great effort to keep his balance, and it was increasingly difficult to keep the long-boards in contact with the snow. He was trying to be cautious but his speed increased. Every time he dragged the pole harder, the less downward pressure he had on the long-boards. His top half was being slowed by the pole but the long-boards wanted to shoot ahead. To keep upright he had to keep his weight centered, which meant he could not use the pole to slow his progress.

He thought of purposely running into a tree with the pole held horizontally in both hands across his chest, so that it would bear the brunt of the impact. He could not see any tree clearly, and at the speed he was going it was going to be difficult to get it right. The speed became frighteningly fast and he could feel he was losing control. His left long-board became airborne, and as he tried to level himself out by bringing his left board down, his right board slipped underneath him and he fell.

The change of direction was immediate; he was now plummeting vertically down the slope. His back was toward the snow and his lower body was caught at right angles to it. As he kept the pole in both hands above his head, he did his best to keep the long-boards downhill of his body. The boards bounced and scraped along the icy surface, sending showers of snow and ice to his face. He worked the pole along his hands, turned his upper torso in line with his lower body, and, with as much force as he could muster, dug the shorter end of the pole into the snow to slow his progress. It worked well enough and gave him time to see that the slope ahead was about to fall away. He was sliding toward a precipice. With one last herculean effort, he dug the pole harder into the snow and stopped his slide.

The pole was now jammed, stuck horizontally in the ice and snow on the side of a sixty degree hill. He was hanging onto the pole, suspended a few feet above where the hill disappeared over an edge into a ravine. His choices were few; any sudden movement might break the pole and send him crashing down into the darkness below. In the ravine there were sure to be rocks, and any fall would cause certain injury. He could try kicking his long-boards off and lift himself up to where he could wrap his legs around the pole and maybe

pull himself to safety. But then he would be without his long-boards and facing a lengthy and treacherous hike out of the mountains. Every second he delayed, his strength would ebb away, and falling would be his only alternative.

The ravine was so deep, that he could barely see beyond the tops of the trees. The trees were probably more than a hundred feet tall, which meant the ravine was probably more than two hundred feet deep. He knew he had to recover quickly before he lost his strength. He tried to swing himself up. There was an audible crack and for a moment he was not sure what had happened. He felt a sudden rush of cold air, as if a freak wind had blown him off the mountain. Everything started to turn. The pole was gone from his hands. Nothing was holding him now, he was in free-fall, and it was exhilarating for a few seconds, until he felt his body hitting a branch of a big pine. The branched slapped him like a baseball bat, but the fall continued and he was slapped and slapped again by subsequent branches. From one branch to another and then another until one of the branches flipped him over, so the next branch hit him powerfully in the face. He was barely conscious by the time his body slammed into the snow at the bottom.

He lay there, slipping in and out of consciousness. He knew he was badly hurt, but there was little blood, only a trickle from his nose. He was lying face up, but one of his legs was bent awkwardly behind his back. He was not sure how long his lucid periods were, but he must have been laying there for some time. Far off he heard a muffled humming sound. A fresh snow had blanketed him from head to foot. As he shook the snow from his face and recovered his senses, pain flooded his body. Despite the pain, the humming noise was more distinct. It was his mobile phone. He tried to pull his pack up and over his head, but a vicious pain shot through the length of his left arm. Using his right hand only, he awkwardly got the pack off his back and fumbled inside for his phone. It was one of his two friends. "Michael, where are you?"

Michael had difficulty talking but he mumbled enough sense to make his friend understand.

He had lost consciousness again. A sustained drone of helicopter blades brought him back to a semi-conscious state. The noise was followed by a bright light. Through his discomfort he was vaguely aware of a helmeted man laying him in a metal stretcher, and then being hoisted out of the ravine.

The next day, in hospital, Michael watched the evening news. The lady on the TV reported, "Three friends have gained a new admiration for their hero Snowshoe Thompson. The young men had to abandon their re-enactment of Thompson's historical long-board run across the Sierras, after one of the men became seriously injured in a fall. The young man was medevac'd to Sacramento's Sutter General Hospital with severe facial bruising, a dislocated shoulder, several cracked ribs, and a broken leg."

The lady reporter turned to a colleague on the news desk and continued, "If it had not been for a mobile phone and a helicopter rescue, this might have ended very differently!"

"Yes indeed," her colleague replied, "Fortunately his friends were able to alert Air and Mountain Rescue. Just imagine what would have happened if he had attempted this foolhardy venture alone?"

The lady smiled at her colleague, "You mean like Snow-shoe Thompson used to do?"

Snowshoe Thompson, courtesy of Nevada Historical Society.

The young Mark Twain

Hank Monk in his winter outfit,
courtesy of Nevada Historical Society

Captain Dick Barter at Emerald Bay
Courtesy California State Library
Not known if this is pre 1870, but proof the Captain was a
gifted craftsman. Author maintains with such skills Dick Barter was unlikely to have just used oars on his weekly shopping excursions.

Pier at Tahoe City ca 1870   *J-14.8*

Tahoe City's Custom House (Campbell's) building on the pier 1870 (according to hand-written note) the site of Jim Stewart death two years later. Believed to be the Steamer Tod Goodwin on the far side of the pier and the Steamer Emerald on the near side. Courtesy of the Nevada State Museum.

On the bridge of the SS *Tahoe*, Capt Ernest John Pomin far left, courtesy of Tahoe City Gate Keeper's Museum.

The locomotive on the narrow gauge of the Lake Tahoe
Railroad which hauled timber up to Spooner Summit from
Glenbrook, during the last quarter of nineteenth century.
Courtesy Nevada State Museum.

Clark Gable, Glenbrook beach, taking time off from waiting tables. Courtesy Tahoe Historical Society.

Friday's Station Pony Bob Haslam's home station. Courtesy Tahoe Historical Society.

Friday's Station today

Carson, Tahoe, Lumber & Fluming Company. The lumber-
yard was a mile long and half a mile wide, located south of
Carson City with a spur of the Virginia Truckee Railroad
running through the middle, V-Flumes are on either side.
Courtesy of the Nevada State Museum.

One of the many medal ceremonies at the Squaw Valley
Olympics (Ski Jump in the background) courtesy of the
Gate Keeper's Museum, Tahoe City.

Backgrounds, Postscripts, Ironies and Controversies.

Some sources of information are often at variance with other sources. It is not a case of considering the source, and it's not always true that the most accurate information is the one most often repeated! Still, there are other accounts out there that are at odds with one another, and I may well be at odds with something else you have read. Did the Indian Truckee die in April or in October 1860? Was Snowshoe Thompson really at the first battle of Pyramid Lake? Did Dick Barter go to South Shore or Tahoe City for his shopping? And was Bill Stewart the last man to shake Lincoln's hand?

I have been as controversial as most, but I try in the following backgrounds and postscripts to be as accurate as possible.

1) Pony Bob Haslam and the Indian Uprising of 1860 (*Solid Gold*)

Haslam's home station, Friday's, still stands today opposite the Edgewood Golf Course on Highway 50; it is the white weatherboard building set back from the road. The property was owned by the Park family for more than a hundred years; sadly is not open to the public. Still, you will see a statue of a young Pony Express rider in full flight outside Harrah's Casino just north of the south shore state line.

The two Indian tribes of western Nevada and eastern California are the Washoe and the Paiutes. The Indians had been helpful to the early white explorers; the Paiute Indian Chief Truckee served as guide to John C. Fremont and Kit Carson during the Pathfinders' two explorations west in the mid-1840s. It was Fremont that commissioned Chief Truckee into the army and gave him the rank of captain. The Indians may have even tried to help the fated Donner Party in 1846, leaving Piñon pine nuts for the settlers to eat. However, suspicion that Indians were intent on poisoning them led the emigrants to ignore their kindness.

The Paiutes had seen many gold prospectors pass through their country during the Californian Gold Rush years. With the discovery of silver in the heart of Indian Territory, a delicate balance was upset. The all-important Piñon pine tree, the staple food for the Indians, was cut down in large numbers by miners, to keep their fires burning. With the situation already strained, the final straw that caused the Paiute Indian uprising in the late spring of 1860 came with the kidnapping of two Indian squaws. The kidnappers were the men of William's Station (a stage and Pony Express station) southeast of Virginia City. The Paiutes attacked, killed the white men, rescued their women, and burned the station to the ground. At the time, Virginia City was a mixture of wooden buildings and tents. Its inhabitants put together a militia consisting of one hundred and five lightly armed men, led by Major Ormsby.

The militia trailed the Indians along the Truckee River toward their main encampment at Pyramid Lake. Four miles before the lake, the Paiutes led by Chief Numaga, were waiting in ambush. At a bend in the river, a group of warriors attacked and the militia retired to a grove of Cottonwood trees. However, many more warriors were in among the Cottonwoods. It is estimated that there were some three hundred Paiutes who took part in what became known as The Massacre of Pyramid Lake. Of the one hundred and five volunteers, seventy-six were killed, including Major Ormsby. And of the surviving twenty-nine, it was believed that no one escaped uninjured. One of the survivors was the famed Snowshoe Thompson.

For a month following the massacre, the whole region was in a state of panic. In June 1860, a second battle of Pyramid Lake was fought, this time an army of eight hundred, including two hundred regular soldiers, met the Paiutes, close to the site of the first battle. Although hailed as a victory by the white settlers, the battle was inconclusive; fatalities were far fewer than in the first battle. The Indians withdrew and the army did not pursue. Killed at the second battle was Captain Storey of the Virginia Rifles.

For a thousand years before the nineteenth century nothing much had changed in the West. Then came the first major expedition with Lewis and Clark in 1804, and before the century was out, everything had change! A whole way of life was turned on its head. In the early years the white settlers needed the Indians' kindness for their survival. By the end of the century the Indians needed the whites' forbearance just to exist. The white settlers justified all they did by labeling the Indians as savages. To dismiss them in such a manner was cruel and unfair. However, to see Indians as naive and peace-loving is to go to the other extreme. Warriors were exactly that: young men who needed to show their prowess in battle. Wars between Indian tribes were numerous. The more aggressive the tribe, the more prosperous it was. When tribes warred against each other, the conquest often went to the tribe with the greater number of horses. In the war with the whites, it was greater fire power that mattered.

Sarah Winnemucca, Truckee's grand-daughter, who received an education and was able to read and write English, was maybe thankful that her grand-father was spared the grief of war. (Ironically, it was at the Ormsby home in Genoa that Sarah learned a good deal of her English.) In her version of the events leading up to the war, the girls kidnapped by the William brothers were only children. However, there are always two sides to any argument. Many settlers thought that William's Station was attacked without provocation. Sarah Winnemucca was to help the United States Army as a mediator in years to come. In a poignant letter she wrote in 1878, she summed up her feelings for her people:-

"My people are ignorant of worldly knowledge, but they know what love means and what truth means. They have seen their dear ones perish around them because their white brothers have given them neither love nor truth. Are not love and truth better than learning? My people have no learning. They do not know anything about the history of the world, but they can see the Spirit Father in everything. The beautiful world talks to them of their Spirit Father. They are innocent and simple, but they are brave and will not be imposed upon. They are patient, but they know black is not white."

Fort Boise, Idaho Territory
August 31st 1878

Postscripts

1) Although not at the two battles of Pyramid Lake, Bob Haslam was wounded twice by the Paiutes. One flint arrow went through his jaw and knocked out three of his teeth.

2) Born in London in 1840, Haslam died in Chicago in 1912. For a while Haslam joined Bill Cody with Sitting Bull in the travelling Buffalo Bill Wild West Show.

3) It is believed Bill Cody (Buffalo Bill) rode for the Pony Express east of the Rockies at the age of fourteen. Despite its place in western folklore, the Pony Express lasted only eighteen months, from April 1860 to October 1861.

4) The month of Captain Truckee's death in 1860 is in dispute. Quite a few accounts suggest that he died in October. However, Sarah Winnemucca claimed that he died in April. Truckee was buried with his captain's commission, written by Fremont, pinned to his chest.

5) Chief Truckee believed that the white settlers were lost brothers and it was the duty of his tribe to reach out to the new settlers in brotherhood. Several local places bear the name of Truckee, including the only river that runs out of Lake Tahoe.

6) Chief Numaga, who led the Paiutes at Pyramid Lake, was like Chief Truckee. He wanted to keep the peace, but he could not appease those warriors who wanted to fight.

7) Virginia City is the county seat of Storey County named after the captain killed at the second battle. His grave can be seen in Virginia City's Boot Hill Cemetery. For many years Carson City sat within Ormsby County, named after the major killed at the first battle.

8) Nothing is more controversial than the meaning of the word Tahoe. Most will tell you it is a Washoe Indian word, but as to its meaning, you will hear a variety of explanations. The most believable is that it comes from the Washoe word for *water's edge* "Da Ow A Ga." The Indians would have understood the first two syllables. Had a lost white man shrugged his shoulders and said "Where is Da Ow?" or even had he said "Where is Ta Ho?" They would have pointed him toward the lake.

2) Old Ben and the Flag over Sonoma
(*The End of an Era*)

Bears are still numerous in the Lake Tahoe Basin. You will see black, brown, cinnamon, and motley-colored bears throughout the area. These are all species of the black bear. A good size male may top three hundred and fifty pounds. They are usually timid and will in most cases run away when they see or smell a human. However, I have known them to be quite indifferent to humans, too. I have on occasion passed within just a few feet of some. Still, these are wild animals, and if you are out camping in the area, they will be emboldened by the chance of a free meal. So be respectful and make sure you leave no food about. Bears are often found near trash cans and inside unsecured dumpsters. On the rare chance one gets aggressive, you should back away slowly or make yourself appear bigger than you are by raising your hands above your head.

Grizzlies will not be intimidated by your raising your hands. A Grizzly male can weigh more than a thousand pounds and can run faster than any human. Anything that challenges a grizzly will come off second best. Even men who have shot and seriously wounded a grizzly have not lived to tell the tale! A male grizzly standing on his hind legs can easily be twice as tall as a human. So, it is perhaps good news, at least for visitors to Lake Tahoe, that there are no grizzly bears left in the Sierra. They were here, but they were all hunted out of existence by the 1920s.

Still, the memory of the grizzly in California is everywhere you go, because of what happened on a June morning in 1846. The United States had been at war with Mexico over the ownership of Texas for more than a month, but the Americans in California may not have known that in June. So it was with some initiative that thirty-three armed rough riders rode into the sleepy town of Sonoma just after dawn on June 14, 1846, under the leadership of William Ide. They pounded on the large door of the Mexican governor's villa on Sonoma Plaza. If they were expecting a fight, they were sadly disappointed. They caught the governor in bed. Mariano Vallejo hurriedly got dressed in military uniform and welcomed his captors. He was sympathetic to their demands, charmed the would-be antagonists, and gave them his best wine from the cellar. The leaders of the bloodless coup were not only victorious but possibly drunk before the night was out!

There was, however, a sense of anti-climax. What had they achieved? Despite being in control of the barracks and having removed the Mexican flag from the plaza, there was no physical evidence that anything of any consequence had taken place. This was supposed to be a new day. What was needed was a new emblem, a new flag. A flag bearing a crude likeness of a grizzly was drawn on a piece of brown muslin. In front of the bear was a red star, beneath the bear were the words "California Republic," and at the base of the flag was a broad red stripe. From that moment on, the action taken in Sonoma on that June day would be known as the Bear Flag Revolt! The new flag was hoisted above the plaza on June 15.

Major John Charles Fremont, who was on his second exploration west in 1846, had just reached California in early June. Although taking no part in the revolt it is believed that the action at Sonoma had Fremont's blessing. Expanding the war in Texas to California was a natural step, and by July the United States had naval ships in the Pacific. On July 5 the Stars and Stripes was flying above the Mexican Customs House in Monterey. Roughly at the same time, the *USS Portsmouth* under the command of Captain Montgomery, sailed to Yerba Buena (San Francisco) and raised the Stars and Stripes in the plaza there, which later became known as Portsmouth Square.

The only problem that bothered both Fremont and Montgomery was the flag at Sonoma. Those troubling words, "California Republic," caused concern to all those that embraced the idea of Manifest Destiny (the belief that all land between the Atlantic and the Pacific was ordained by God to be part of a greater union.) An independent California was not to be tolerated. Captain Montgomery sent a small attachment of men from the *USS Portsmouth*, including his own son, with the sole purpose of replacing the rebel flag with the Stars and Stripes. So it was that, on July 9, the rebels at Sonoma watched passively as their Bear Flag was taken down and replaced by Old Glory. California was now an integral part of the greater war against Mexico. Besides Fremont, Commodore Robert Stockton and General Stephen Kearney would soon be leading the American cause in the west.

For a while Mariano Vallejo was imprisoned at Sutter's Fort near present-day Sacramento. John Sutter treated the ex-governor as a Californios (a native of California) rather than as a Mexican prisoner. Fremont was annoyed that Sutter, an American, should treat the prisoner with such civil hospitality. Still, Vallejo also considered himself a Californios and supported the takeover of California, preferring the Americans to the Russians, British, French, Spanish, and Mexicans.

Four years after the Bear Flag Revolt, California became a state. At the state's five-year anniversary, in 1855, the original flag that had flown over Sonoma nine years earlier was paraded through the streets of San Francisco. Proud to be part of the Union and no longer posing a threat of independence, everyone viewed the Bear Flag affectionately.

Some fifty years later, the Bear Flag was adopted as the California State Flag. The flag was little altered except that the bear was redrawn to show the familiar gait of the grizzly with its hunched shoulder. By 1911 the flag was flying over all government buildings throughout the state. Even though the bear was redrawn the flag still bears the defiant words "California Republic."

Postscripts

1) Some locals report seeing black bears of upwards of six hundred pounds and I believe one Alaskan grizzly weighed close to sixteen hundred pounds.

2) The original Bear Flag was lost in the San Francisco Earthquake and Fire of 1906. It was the Mexican governor Vallejo who remarked that the original drawing on the flag looked more like a pig than a bear.

3) It was Charles Nahl's drawing of the grizzly that was adopted as the bear you see on today's state flag. The original bear on the Sonoma flag was drawn by William L. Todd a relative of Mary Todd (who married Abraham Lincoln.)

4) Vallejo went onto serve in the state legislature. The city of Vallejo, at the northern end of the San Francisco Bay, is named after him.

5) Caught in a power struggle between Kearney and Stockton, Fremont was appointed California Military Governor by Stockton. The appointment was dismissed by Kearney, and Fremont was unjustly court-martialed by the army for insubordination. President Polk later rescinded all the charges. Fremont went on to become the first Republican Candidate to run for president in 1856, but lost to James Buchanan.

6) Fremont was the first documented white explorer to view Lake Tahoe on Valentine's Day, 1844.

3) Mark Twain, the Duel between North and South and the prize of Virginia City. (*The Immortal Faces Death*)

Except for the first three months of the Civil War, Samuel Clemens (Mark Twain) spent most of the war years in the west, the majority of that time he spent in Virginia City. At the start of the war he spent a brief two weeks in the Missouri Militia, but he and his men gave way when they heard that Union troops were searching for them.

Like many, Twain was not always convinced what side he was on in the Civil War. In his early years he had never thought of slavery as wrong; it was just something he had grown up with. In later years, he would change his tune and consider it a blot on the nation's character. He came out west in June or July of 1861, with his brother Orion. Orion Clemens was ten years older, and there was no mistaking what side the older brother had chosen. He had even campaigned for Lincoln's presidency. It was not unexpected that Orion would be chosen for a political office, and so it was that Orion was offered the post of Secretary of State for the new Nevada Territory.

The Territory of Nevada was created out of what was the western half of Utah Territory, on March 2, 1861. Up until then, Utah Territory had been governed by Brigham Young, the Mormon leader. It may be possible that Washington and the silver miners did not want the wealth of Virginia City falling into Mormon hands, so Washington D.C., hurriedly created the new Nevada Territory. The Mormon population of the local area was already in decline, due to Brigham Young calling all Mormons back from the outlying settlements, in

1857 to defend Salt Lake City against possible attack by federal troops. A lasting peace between Washington and the Mormons would not come until the building of the Transcontinental Railroad in 1868.

Mark Twain recounts his journey out west and his adventures in the Tahoe area in his book *Roughing It.* He came under the premise that he was going to help his older brother and would call himself the Secretary's secretary, but it was an unpaid job and Sam could not make a living in Carson City. Carson City became the administrative center for the new territory and, in 1864, would become the state capital. Young Sam, attracted by the possibility of making a fortune in mining, soon found himself looking for a claim. Eventually, he would end up in Virginia City and would write an article or two for the local newspapers. His brother Orion had once owned the *Hannibal Western Union,* and Sam may have written an occasional article for his brother's paper.

After a brief love affair with mining, young Sam was happier writing and he accepted a job as reporter for *The Territorial Enterprise* at twenty-five dollars a week. It was a princely sum of money for a man previously unpaid. It was as a reporter that Sam believed he had finally found his true vocation. Having earned his pilot's license on the paddle steamers of the Mississippi, he adopted the pen-name Mark Twain. As a measurement, *mark twain* meant: "two fathoms deep" or "safe water for a paddle steamer to negotiate the river." The idea that the news was safe in Mark Twain's hands proved to be a misnomer.

The truth may have only been distorted by Twain's pen, but the health of Lake Tahoe was certainly not safe in his hands. During his time in Virginia City, Mark came to the

lake a few times and he was beguiled by her. Giving expres
sion to chosen words, he declared "that three months of camp
life on Lake Tahoe would restore an Egyptian mummy to his
pristine vigor and give him an appetite like an alligator." He
felt so exhilarated by the beauty, the air, and the clarity of
the lake that he and his friend Johnny decided to build a
cabin and make claim to some lake shore frontage. They got
as far as cutting one log, before deciding to make a less substantial affair and build it out of branches. After some effort
they decided that it didn't necessarily have to be square. So
they began a tepee made out of smaller branches and foliage.
Having worked for an hour or two, Mark built a camp fire to
make some coffee and went to fetch some lake water.

He returned to see the manzanita on fire and their tepee
collapsed into a blackened heap. He and his friend were
transfixed, watching the fire spread from bush to bush, from
bush to tree, from tree to tree. Blown by the breeze, it went
up the slope to the ridge, along the ridge, up another slope
and to another ridge. It went up and over several ridges, ignit-
ing everything as it went. It then spread to the neighboring
canyon, a bright orange glow weaving its way steadily up the
mountain. Eventually it disappeared over the mountain and
out of sight. Exhausted by this marvelous spectacle, the two
went to sleep on the beach four hours later.

Bill Stewart, one of the two original state senators for
Nevada, described Mark Twain as a scoundrel who would
surely deserve a hanging someday. Stewart came to Virginia
City at the time of the Indian Troubles in 1860. He became a
much needed litigation lawyer for mining rights on the Comstock. When silver veins ran horizontally for many feet underground, there were many disputes between adjacent mining companies over rights to mine the vein. Many disputes

st fights and strong-arm tactics. Stewart had many
and became the lawyer of choice for many of the
sputes. Stewart was fiercely pro-Union and highly
delighted when Nevada became a new territory.

A few short weeks after the birth of Nevada, the nation was
at war with itself; the wealth of Virginia City had the possibility
to turn the tide for either side. Certainly Washington did not
want the wealth falling into the hands of the Confederacy, but
Virginia City had its fair share of southern sympathizers. Opposing Stewart on one rights case was the infamous Judge David S.
Terry, who had once been the Californian Chief Justice.

"Texan Terry" had been an advocate for the extension of
slavery in California. He had to escape from San Francisco in
1859 after he killed the popular Free Soil state senator David
Broderick in a duel. It was Terry's choice of weapons and he
had selected a pair of hair-triggered pistols. Broderick, ignorant of the pistol's sensitive action, discharged his weapon
prematurely without ever aiming it. The many onlookers
thought Terry would do the honorable thing and harmlessly
fire his weapon into the air, but sadly he chose to put a bullet
through the senator's left lung.

Stewart and the Union had a few other opponents on the
Comstock. A local chapter of the mysterious but pro-southern Knights of the Golden Circle was formed in Virginia City
by a Doctor Selden McMeans, and it claimed a membership
of more than two hundred by the spring of 1861. McMeans
boasted that he intended to attack Fort Churchill with a hundred men and capture it for the Confederacy. It proved to be
an idle threat and McMeans was soon to find out that Fort
Churchill's commanding officer was not one to be taken
lightly.

There was also Virginia City's prosecuting attorney, Patrick Henry Clayton, a sworn secessionist. Still, Stewart had many supporters too, not least of which were the men of the Virginia City fire station, who, like Bill Stewart, were all from New York.

After the southern victory at Bull Run, members of the Golden Circle hoisted the confederate flag above Newman's saloon on Virginia City's A Street. On hearing the news of Bull Run, the firefighters spilled onto the streets and started fighting with any southern sympathizers they found. Fort Churchill, on the Carson River a few miles south-east of Virginia City, had been built a year earlier as a direct result of the Paiute Indian War. The commanding officer, Captain Joseph Stewart (no relation to Bill Stewart) was at Alcatraz at the time of the first battle of Pyramid Lake. It had been his idea to turn the island of Alcatraz into a military prison. He now wanted to turn Fort Churchill into a prison for southern sympathizers. On hearing of the confederate flag raised in Virginia City, Captain Stewart led an attachment of soldiers to take it down. It was already down by the time he arrived.

The southern sympathizers were badly outnumbered on the Comstock. Judge Terry was never well liked, although it was said Bill Stewart had a grudging respect for him. Terry abandoned the struggle to win the silver wealth for the South and went back to Texas to form his own regiment. The likes of McMeans and Clayton were overshadowed. Bill Stewart became a civic leader, and through his influence Carson City, not Virginia City, became the State Capitol. A lot of the wealth of the Comstock went to help the North, and a grateful Abraham Lincoln rewarded the territory by proposing that Nevada become a state.

On October 31st 1864, before the end of the Civil War and three and a half short years after it became a territory, Nevada became the thirty-sixth state to join the Union. Even the onetime Missouri Militia man started to wax lyrical about the Union. So much so that Mark Twain became the driving force behind the writing of General Grant's memoirs and personally sponsored their publication in 1885. General Grant died thirteen days after he had dictated the last page to Mark Twain.

Postscripts

1) Mark Twain went travelling to the Holy Land and had the idea to write a book (his first book) of his experiences. It was called "Innocents Abroad", and was published in 1869. He wrote most of the book while as a guest at Bill Stewart's residence in Washington, D.C

2) Twain claimed that he was with General Tom Harris of the Missouri Militia at the time Ulysses S. Grant arrived in Florida, Missouri, with Union troops. However, this would have put Twain in Missouri when we believe he was already on a stage headed west.

3) Lake Tahoe's official name for many years was Lake Bigler named after the third governor of California. The once-popular governor made himself unpopular by supporting the southern cause during the Civil War.

4) Bill Stewart is proudly remembered by Nevadans as the last man to shake Abraham Lincoln's hand. The senator had stopped by the White House to introduce a colleague, but Lincoln told him to come back at ten the next morning, because he was just off to the theater.

5) Warner Brothers made a Western called *"Virginia City"* in 1940 about the struggle for the town's wealth at the time of the Civil War. The movie was not a great success, even though it starred Errol Flynn and Humphrey Bogart.

6) The *"Bonanza"* TV Series had an episode called "The War comes to Washoe." Two of the characters in the episode were Bill Stewart and Judge Terry.

7) There is a museum in Havana, Cuba, that had two Mark Twain skulls on display. One skull when he was a child and the other when he was an adult. (Twain would have been delighted by both exhibits!)

8) Nevada is the only state that has Halloween as a state holiday.

4) The Chinese & the Railroad (*Jung Lo*)

The Jung Lo story is fictitious but the Chinese contribution to building of the Central Pacific can only be understated.

In a time after my story is set, it became a common practice to sink vertical shafts down from the exterior granite rock and build tunnels from the inside out. Pushing in opposite directions from within toward the headings, this would have left the guess work out of whether the tunnels were aligned or not. This would have also provided constant shelter from the elements and removed the need to clear snow. On the other hand, the explosions within a confined space may have been even more dangerous. It is hard to imagine that the Chinese were continually retreating up the narrow shaft each time charges were primed and lighted. The estimated number of Chinese who worked on the Central Pacific Railroad varied anywhere from fifteen to twenty-five thousand.

The Union Pacific, working west from Omaha, employed many men who had drifted west after the horrors of the Civil War. As the Union Pacific inched westwards, a series of sin camps attached themselves to the ever-moving end of the line. There was no shortage of liquor, con men, and prostitutes. Gambling and fighting were commonplace, keeping the men sober and on the job was a perpetual headache. There were no such problems with the industrious Chinese; they never fought, were tee-total and although gambling is a favorite Chinese pastime, they entrusted their money to chosen guardians from among their own.

In October 1865, an interesting report was written by Leland Stanford (president of the Central Pacific) to President Andrew Johnson, regarding the employment of the Chinese as railroad laborers. In the report below, Stanford seems to be justifying the employment of the Chinese, which may indicate that Johnson probably had some concerns over so much foreign employment:-

"As a class they are quiet, peaceable, patient, industrious and economical. Ready and apt to learn all the different kinds of work required in railroad building, they soon become as efficient as white laborers. More prudent and economical, they are contented with less wages. We find them organized into societies for mutual aid and assistance. These societies can count their numbers by the thousands, are conducted by shrewd, intelligent business men who promptly advise their subordinates where employment can be found on most favorable terms. No system similar to slavery, serfdom or peonage prevails among these laborers. Their wages, which are always paid in coin each month, are divided among them by their agents who attend to their business according to the labor done by each person. Their agents are generally American or Chinese merchants who furnish them supplies of food, the value of which they deduct from their monthly pay."

Leland Stanford, Sacramento
October, 1865

Leland Stanford, Collis Huntington, Mark Hopkins and Charles Crocker were the founders of the Central Pacific and known as the Big Four. It was Huntington who had gone to listen to young railroad engineer Theodore Judah give a lecture on a possible railroad across the continent. Judah had been the chief engineer on the first railroad of the Pacific Coast from Sacramento to Folsom. It had been this young engineer who surveyed the original route for the Transcontinental Railroad. Although taken aboard by the four associates as chief engineer, Judah was unhappy that too much attention was placed on speed of construction rather than on quality. On his way to Washington, D.C., via Panama, possibly to look for new investors to buy the Big Four out, Judah contracted Yellow Fever. He died in 1863, at the age of thirty-seven. Judah was subsequently proven right, because much of the railroad had to be reconstructed over the following sixty years.

Postscripts

1) Mian Situ's painting *The Powder Monkeys – Cape Horn – 1865*, shows the Chinese working a year before the Jung Lo story. Jung Lo came to work when the Chinese had already progressed just short of the summit. Mian Situ's painting is of the building of the railroad bed around a rocky precipice above the north fork of the American River, just east of present day Colfax. This rocky precipice was nicknamed Cape Horn, because it presented a challenge to get around, just as the sailing around Cape Horn was for nineteenth-century sailors.

2) It is author's opinion: that going through the granite rock of Donner Summit was the most challenging part of the Transcontinental Railroad. The part around Cape Horn was certainly a challenge too, but at an elevation of 2500 feet

(as opposed to Donner Summit's elevation above 7,000 feet) there was very little in the way of snow at Cape Horn. Still, as shown in Mian Situ's painting there was a near-vertical drop of thirteen hundred feet into the American river, it marvelously shows the intrepid Chinese as they go about their work chipping out a railroad bed.

3) There were quite a few Chinese in California before the railroad. They had been gold mining the Sierra foothills in the early 1850s. The Placer County population in 1852 was estimated at just over ten thousand; more than three thousand were Chinese.

4) Leland Stanford went onto become California governor and the first locomotive of the Central Pacific was named "*The Governor Stanford.*" He also founded Stanford University as a memorial to his son, and went on to serve in the US Senate.

5) On May 10th 1869, the Central Pacific met the Union Pacific at Promontory Point, Utah, and the journey from coast to coast was reduced from a matter of months to a matter of days. Of course, it was Leland Stanford who hammered in the Golden Spike.

6) Fifty years later in 1919, it was decided that the two railroads met at Promontory Summit and not at Promontory Point. Promontory Point and Promontory Summit are about thirty miles apart. This has caused some confusion, but experts now say that the railroads met about a mile west of Promontory Summit.

7) The Virginia Truckee Railroad built, from 1869 to 1872, joined the Comstock silver mines and Carson City to the Transcontinental Railroad. Running south from Reno through

the Washoe Valley to Carson City, it was the VT Railroad that hauled cut timber up to Virginia City.

8) In the 1870s, there was mass unemployment through-out San Francisco and anti-Chinese sentiment grew violent, as the immigrants were accused of taking jobs from the white workers.

9) In 1882, President Chester A. Arthur signed the Chinese Exclusion Act, which postponed any further Chinese immigration and denied the Chinese rights to US citizenship; the Act was not repealed until 1943.

10) One of Lake Tahoe's earliest steamers was also named *The Governor Stanford.*

5) The Flooding of the Comstock and the Sutro Tunnel (*The Hole in the Lake*)

The inventive story of "The Mystery of the Savage Sump," (the original name for the story) first appeared in 1901. Sam Davis got his inspiration for the story having heard a rumor of a hole in the lake. In all likelihood there is no hole in Lake Tahoe, but it was a fact that the mine shafts of Virginia City used to flood. Some of the mine shafts were sunk horizontally into the side of the mountain, and others went straight down. Those mines that went the deepest had less air, less light, more stress on the supporting timbers, more chance of cave-ins, a greater chance for explosions and a greater chance for flooding! Flooding was a particular problem for the Savage Mine, because at more than two thousand feet, it was the deepest mine on the Comstock.

So where did all the water come from? No, it did not come from Lake Tahoe (well at least not directly.) There is only one outlet for Lake Tahoe, and that is the Truckee River. The Truckee River flows out of the lake at Tahoe City, flows north for fourteen miles, and then makes a right-hand turn just before it reaches the town of Truckee. It flows east for another sixty miles through the town of Reno and then makes a left-hand turn and flows north to Pyramid Lake......., a distance of a hundred and fifteen miles from beginning to end. Pyramid Lake, thirty-three miles northeast of Reno, has no out-flowing river. This situation is repeated all over Northern Nevada: lakes with no out-flowing rivers, or rivers that just disappear into the ground. Both the Carson and Humboldt Rivers flow into their respective sinks; none of the local rivers flow to the sea. Northern Nevada is part of the Great Basin, not because it looks like one but because it acts like one!

It was the natural underground water that flooded the silver mines. With geothermal activity throughout the local area, this was quite often hot or even scalding water. A five-mile tunnel was built by Adolph Sutro to drain all the flooded mine shafts; it was built at the base of Mount Davidson, underneath the Comstock, at 1750 feet below the surface. As the water funneled its way out of the tunnel, it then found its natural way to the Carson River. Water which flooded the even deeper Savage Mine was collected into an excavated sump and was pumped up to the Sutro tunnel.

Postscripts

1) At the time of "Hole in the Lake" story, Carnelian Bay on Tahoe's northwest shore was known as Cornelian Bay, after the blue cornelian stones once found there.

2) Nevada's Mount Davidson is the highest peak in the Virginia Hills, at 7,864 feet. California's Mount Davidson is also the highest peak in the San Francisco Hills, at 938 feet. Ironically, it was Adolph Sutro who planted trees on Mount Davidson in San Francisco.

3) It was estimated the Sutro tunnel drained four million gallons of water a day. It not only drained water but provided much- needed ventilation to the lower mine shafts. The five mile tunnel took nine years to complete from 1869 to 1878.

4) Adolph Sutro went on to become San Francisco mayor from 1894 to 1896. An avid reader, Sutro built up a magnificent library of more than three hundred thousand books, considered to be one of four best libraries in America in the late 1890s.

5) In 1896, Sutro built the best remembered version of the Cliff House (The Gingerbread Palace) overlooking the Pacific Ocean, just south of San Francisco,

6) In conjunction with the Cliff House, Sutro opened the famous Sutro Baths. Advertised as the largest salt water natatorium in the world!

7) Sutro died in 1898. Fortunately he was spared some grief. Part of his library was destroyed in the Earthquake and Fire of 1906. In 1907, the Gingerbread Cliff House burned down and in 1966, the Sutro Baths burned down.

6) Emerald Bay (*Three-Toed Island*)

I have taken the liberty to mention the island in the title, yet hardly mention it in the story, and I apologize for this.

After his near-death experience in 1870 Captain Dick built a small wooden tomb for himself on the island at the bay. Had I continued my story to the demise of Richard Barter, you would have learned that the captain repeated his folly of that winter's night three years later. He had gone shopping for vittles' and returned again into the teeth of another storm. But sadly, that night in 1873, he was lost. His friends found wreckage of the boat he called *The Nancy,* and (I like to say) in among the wreckage they found the three pickled toes. But most of our beloved captain sunk to Lake Tahoe's bottom. His friends interred the toes in the tomb on the island and therefore you have the title of the story.

Some would have you believe that Dick Barter did not sail but rowed the boat all the way to the Tahoe House in Tahoe City. This would have been an extraordinary thing for the Captain to have even contemplated in the winter. The round-trip distance to Tahoe City from Emerald Bay by boat is well in excess of thirty miles. A captain used to sailing round the Horn and having lived at Tahoe for many years would not have treated our lady with such little regard to her foul tempers. He may have been drunk on his return journeys but we have no reason to believe he would have started his weekly expeditions in that state. Anyway, I have set my story, as I have always done, with the captain *sailing* his boat to the south shore. With a prevailing westerly wind, the Captain would have made good use of the sail, certainly on the outbound journey.

Leaving the conjecture aside, this is a true story. The captain was a very sociable hermit. He had at least three dogs, plus the bald eagle to keep him company during his periods of solitude. Despite all those hours spent alone, we believe the captain enjoyed the company of his fellow man. He must have felt he was truly blessed, waking up to the sight of the bay every morning. It is hard to feel lonely when you live so close to God. With a cathedral of surrounding granite, and its own alter made of rock rising up from the middle of an emerald-green floor, he was as close to paradise as any mortal could have been. It was not until 1913, that the road was completed around Emerald Bay, and the bay would then become one of the most photographed places in the country.

In the 1920s, Laura Josephine Knight fell in love with the bay. Thinking the bay was also an image of Valhalla, she had her own *Viking's Home* built on the bay's shoreline. This wealthy lady, we are reliably told, was the main sponsor for Charles Lindbergh's 1927 solo flight across the Atlantic in the Spirit of Saint Louis aircraft.

The bay was used as the setting for the "Indian Love Call," between Nelson Eddy and Jeanette MacDonald in the 1936 film *Rose Marie*. It is said the ghost of *Rose Marie* can still be heard singing for her lost lover, when the wind moans around the bay. And when Rose Marie sings too loudly she can bring the mountain down. This is why the road is often closed during bad winter weather, the road is susceptible to rock slides and avalanches, Two big slides occurred in 1954 and 1967; the earlier slide closed the road for eighteen months.

Postscripts

1) Most often called Fanette island, the island has had several other names. It is sometimes call Deadman's Island after the captain.

2) The shell of Laura Knight's tea house is the small stone structure on top of the island. Captain Dick's wooden tomb survived for a short while but has now totally disappeared. Emerald Bay is now California state property. *The Viking's Home* is open for tours during the summer season.

3) The state marker at the bay, "The Hermit of Emerald Bay" dedicated to Dick Barter, states that Barter rowed all the way to Tahoe City, and also that he only amputated two of his toes. (This is still disputed by your author.)

7) Jim Stewart and the Timber-Cutting Days (*The Dreaded Evening Drink*)

Tahoe City's Trail End Cemetery is located just behind Tahoe City's golf course. Jim Stewart's grave is a simple one; its inscription reads "Jim Stewart Outlaw killed in gunfight at Tahoe City 1872."

We do not know much about Jim Stewart other than he was a lumberjack and he was paid extra money to work alone. His nickname "The Silent Terror" was possibly due to his unprovoked anger toward others. A lot of disaffected men came out west after the Civil War. A few had an understandable bitterness over the turmoil and ruin of their previous lives. The fact that there were people like Jim Stewart was not amazing. It's probably more amazing that there were not more men like him. Still, the West had much to offer men who were leaving the horrors of war and seeking a chance at a new life. Those that missed out on the Gold Rush had the opportunity of employment on the railroads, in the silver mines, or cutting timber. Being a lumberjack around Lake Tahoe would have been preferable for many of these men.

There are more than six hundred miles of tunnels beneath Virginia City, and every few feet there were Tahoe timber supports shoring the shafts up from possible cave-ins. Tens of thousands of Douglas fir, Jeffrey, Ponderosa, Lodgepole and Sugar pines were cut, hauled, shipped, and shaped at Lake Tahoe for the Virginia City silver mines. All types of conveyance were used in the transporting of lumber from ox wagon to steamer and from train to flume. Without Tahoe lumber, the fortune that came out of Comstock could not have been mined. Systematically, acre by acre, the hills and mountains of Lake Tahoe were laid bare.

It was a vast operation and there were several different lumber companies in the Tahoe area during the last quarter of the nineteenth century. However, by far the biggest lumber operation was that of the Carson Tahoe, Lumber and Fluming Company, at Glenbrook owned by Duane Leroy Bliss. For his lumber company, Bliss bought up tracks of land on three sides of the lake. He remarkably bought Meeks Bay, on the west shore, for as little as $250. The best solution to get the cut timber from the south and west shores of Lake Tahoe was to bring it down to the water. Ox wagons were used to get the felled trees to the water's edge, the cut timbers were then floated on the lake, chained, and towed over to Glenbrook.

Several steamers were used to tow the logs over the lake. Among them were the *SS Truckee*, the *SS Emerald* and the *SS Meteor* (the launching of which was mentioned in the book's introduction.) In the Glenbrook sawmills, the timber was cut and shaped. Prior to 1875 the logs were hauled to Spooner Summit by ox wagons. In the late 1860s, a series of V flumes, fed by water from Marlette Lake, were built to carry logs and cut timber down to Carson City. Running twelve miles down the Carson Range, the flumes dropped two hundred feet in every mile of flume. The logs reached an average speed of sixty miles an hour as they rushed along the churning water inside.

When the Virginia Truckee Railroad was opened in the 1870s, they built a railroad spur to the Carson Tahoe Lumber and Fluming Company's massive lumber yard to the south of Carson City. Some of the timber would go straight to Virginia City via the VT Railroad. Some of it would be taken to the planing mill in Carson City. From the moment a tree was felled on Tahoe's west shore, it might have been hauled a mile or so by ox wagon to the water's edge, towed fifteen miles across the lake by steamer, milled at one of the Glenbrook mills, then taken nearly nine miles up the mountain by the Lake Tahoe Railroad to Spooner Summit, carried twelve miles by V flume down to the valley, and then onward another nineteen miles by the Virginia Truckee Railroad to the Comstock. By the time the silver mining came to an end in 1890s, an estimated 750 million feet of board was taken up to Virginia City.

Postscripts

1) There is the amusing account, written by H.J Ramsdell, a reporter for *The New York Tribune*, of possibly the first ever flume ride. Ramsdell in the company of two of the millionaire owners of the Virginia Consolidated Mine, Jim Fair and James Flood, rode the flume of the Pacific Wood Lumber and Fluming Company and barely lived to tell the tale. Ramsdell said he was so terrified, that he gripped the sides of the purposely built V boat, so tightly that he was picking out wooden splinters from his hands for a whole week.

2) Philip Deidesheimer developed the interlocking square set, which made the mines' supporting timbers several times stronger. It required precise cutting to make the interlocking ends fit tightly. This would have been done after the timber had come down the flume, at the planing mill in Carson City. The *Bonanza* series had an episode called "The Philip Deidesheimer Story."

3) A lumberjack's wife, complained to Reno tailor Jacob (Youphes) Davis that her husband's overalls tore too often at the pockets. Overalls were usually made of cotton duck cloth, the same material Jacob used for tents and covered wagons. Jacob discovered that, by using copper rivets, he could make the material much stronger. Jacob asked his supplier Levi Strauss if he was interested in making overalls with copper rivets. Davis and Strauss patented the idea and Davis joined Strauss in San Francisco. Later they used a softer cotton-twill from France, called *Serge de Nimes*; in time *de Nimes* would get shortened to denim. Levi jeans did not have belt hoops until 1922.

4) The Carson Tahoe Lumber and Fluming Company's lumber yard outside Carson City, stretched more than a mile in length and more than half a mile across (see photo.)

5) In 1875, Duane Leroy Bliss beat the two Murphy brothers to the purchase of Meeks Bay on Tahoe's west shore. The brothers had intended to establish a dairy farm there. Mr. Bliss told the brothers he would resell the bay back to them, once he taken the timber. This he did, and the Murphy brothers were able to buy the bay for the same price $250.

6) In 1898, after the timber-cutting days were over, the railroad up to Spooner Summit was dismantled and transported across the lake on barges. It was re-laid and extended along the Truckee River Canyon between Tahoe City and Truckee. Passengers could now come straight off the Transcontinental and continue by train down to the Tahoe Tavern pier.

7) In 1926, the Southern Pacific took over the lease of the Lake Tahoe Railway and changed the track to standard gauge, buying the railroad outright in 1933. The Southern Pacific

operated the train service another ten years before the rail was torn up and went to help the war effort, in 1943.

8) The age-old question "when a tree falls down in the forest and there is no one there to hear it, does it make a sound?" - is unanswerable. However, if someone is there to hear and the tree is a big Ponderosa or a Douglas fir, it makes enough noise to wake the dead!

Hank and Horace (The Greeley Story)

It is doubtful we will ever know the truth of the Greeley Story.

It was immortalized by two icons of American literature. Mark Twain (America's favorite author) and Artemus Ward (Abraham Lincoln's favorite author) both supported the theory that Greeley had fallen prey to the mischievous Monk.

On the other hand, we have a silent Horace Greeley. Greeley was a political hot potato, a crusader of radical ideas, and one of the founders of the Liberal Republican party. That Greeley was hung out for ridicule was not surprising; his campaign to expose corruption threatened many in Washington. As the editor and founder of the *New York Tribune* he was a powerful man. Had he been elected president he would have been to his many enemies a powerfully *dangerous* man.

How dangerous? If you take it to the extreme, you can almost say that Horace Greeley helped give birth to communism. Karl Marx and Friedrich Engels both wrote articles for the New York Tribune. Marx was a regular contributor from London. For all this, Horace Greeley was popular, his paper had the largest distribution in the nation, and, as a fierce abolitionist Greeley views were initially embraced by Abraham Lincoln.

Is there any truth to the Greeley story? The only doubt cast is that when Greeley (obviously as a newspaper man) wrote about his journey west in *An Overland Journey from New York to San Francisco 1859,* Hank Monk is not mentioned by name. He writes of his stagecoach journeys only in general terms, although he does praise the ability of one unnamed stagecoach driver in California.

Now, as much as we want to believe Mark Twain and Artemus Ward, we have to admit that they both tended to exaggerate in the telling of stories. Artemus Ward traveled the country giving tongue-in-cheek one-man shows. Mark Twain and Artemus Ward met in Virginia City and there was an immediate connection between the two of them. Possibly, Twain gave his own slant to a story told to him by Artemus.

In Twain's version, he and his brother are on their journey west when they are told the story of Monk and Greeley. The amusing tale delights Mark Twain at first hearing, but the story is repeated ad nauseam by every new passenger that joins their stage journey. What grinds on Twain's nerves is that the story is not just repeated, it is repeated verbatim. When a new passenger is just about to repeat the tale for a fifth time, Mark Twain begs the would-be story teller not to recount it. The newcomer gets so morose at not being allowed to tell the story that he dies, leaving Twain wrought with guilt.

Mark Twain writes this amusing anecdote in his 1872 book *Roughing It.* Twain makes the anecdote relevant because he and his brother Orion are supposed to be on the same road that Monk and Greeley traveled two years earlier. This cannot be true, however, because Twain and his brother were bound for Carson City. Twain did not travel further west for another three and a half years.

Artemus Ward's version is even more bizarre, because Artemus has Monk and Greeley on a stage traveling east from Folsom to Placerville, with the amusing incident of the would-be escort occurring in Mud Springs, which is west of Placerville. You do not drive through Mud Springs if you are coming from Carson City.

The stagecoach ride of Monk and Greeley is commemorated in the town of Placerville by a historical marker stating that Monk and Greeley came from Carson City. This fits in with Greeley's own journal, even though he does not mention anything of having been thrown around by our stagecoach hero.

So, what is the truth? Of course, had the embarrassing event actually happened, Greeley probably would not have wanted it remembered. He would have played it down and dismissed it as pure fiction, but unfortunately for him the story did do the rounds. It was probably distorted, added to, and exaggerated.

I have given the impression that Monk was reluctant to talk about the Greeley episode, but that might not have been the case. Monk was indeed given a gold watch, which he was obviously proud of, inscribed by the distinguished leaders of the Nevadan community in remembrance of the Greeley ride. Ironically, one of the signatures on the watch belongs to George Hearst, father of newspaper magnate William Randolph Hearst.

Greeley was originally a Whig and then joined the newly created Republican Party in the 1850's. He supported Fremont's nomination for President in 1856. He was outspoken in his opposition to Democrats (even though in the election of 1872 the Democrats supported the Liberal Republican nominee.) One of Greeley's best-known quotes was "All Innkeepers are Democrats" which was quite often misquoted as "All Democrats are innkeepers."

Monk was indeed the son of an innkeeper and he would have taken great delight in telling Greeley so. Despite his seemingly common background, Monk could indeed trace his lineage back (even though we encounter two illegitimate births) to nobility; this would have caused no end of merriment had it been widely known at the time (see below.)

There is enough evidence to confirm that Hank Monk was a loveable but incorrigible rogue. He drove a stage for more than thirty years, and it was a considerable art to maneuver a stage and horses over mountain trails in any kind of weather. We have to believe that Monk knew what he was doing, drunk or sober. That he is not better remembered now in the twenty-first century is sad indeed. His grave is mostly forgotten and indeed the original headstone fell over.

For the World's Fair in Saint Louis in 1904, each state in the union sent various exhibits. Nevada sent, as two of its main exhibits, Hank Monk's stagecoach and Hank Monk's watch.

Postscripts

1) *Roughing It* achieved one of the highest readerships of any book ever printed. Frank Borman and James Lovell read the book out loud while hurtling around the Earth in *Gemini Seven*.

2) Joe Goodman recounts the story of when Artemus took the staff of *The Territorial Enterprise* (including Twain) to dinner at

Chaumond's French restaurant. Before dinner, Artemus stood up with a glass of wine in hand to make a toast: "Gentleman, I give you Upper Canada." Everyone stood up and solemnly drank the toast. A little later Goodman asked Artemus why he had given Upper Canada as the toast, and quite off-handedly Artemus said, "Because I do not want it for myself."

3) Hank Monk, as stated, was born in Waddington, New York, the son of George Wagner Monk, an innkeeper who was likely the illegitimate son of Sir James Monk (1745 -1826,) the chief justice for Lower Canada. Sir James Monk was the grandson of George Monk, who was the illegitimate son of George Monck, the First Earl of Albemarle (1608-1670,) a favorite of both King Charles and his son King Charles II, Monck also found favor with the Lord Protector, Oliver Cromwell. The earl is buried in London's Westminster Abbey.

4) Monk died in February, 1883. J. A. Yerington said that Hank Monk was born in March, 1826, which meant that he died a month before his fifty-seventh birthday. His headstone says he was fifty years old.

5) It was always the intention of the locals to remember Hank Monk with a memorial or a statue somewhere along Kings Canyon. Somehow it was forgotten, or the thought died with a generation. With the building of the new Highway 50, up to Spooner Summit, a statue to Hank Monk on the canyon trail would not be seen by most travelers today.

6) Mr. Sharkey Begovic erected a new headstone above Hank Monk's grave. This highly commendable act of remembrance still omits the fact that Monk was immortalized by the likes of Mark Twain and Artemus Ward.

7) Greeley was nominated Liberal Republican candidate for president and ran against incumbent Ulysses S. Grant in the 1872 election. Greeley died after the election but before the Electoral College had cast their votes. It was a comfortable victory for Grant but Greeley ended up with 43 percent of the popular vote.

8) It was Cassius Marcellus Clay, a co-founder of the Liberal Republican party, who put Greeley's name forward to be the party's nominee for president. Earlier in his political life, Clay had put forward his own Proclamation of Emancipation, which was largely adopted by Abraham Lincoln. Making enemies on the way for his abolitionist stance, Clay (being good with a Bowie knife) had to defend himself physically on more than one occasion. In 1912 an African-American boy whose last name was Clay was given the Christian names Cassius Marcellus, and he in turn gave the names to his son thirty years later. The son, ironically, became quite a good fighter too!

Hank Monk's Epitaph
(written shortly after his death, by the people of Carson City.)

"The Whitest, Biggest-Hearted and Best-Known
Stage Driver of the West,
Who was Kind to All and Thought Ill of None."

Ode to Hank Monk

Monk used to drive the Grade, when the Grade was just a trail.
But he'd bring the stage over on time, and seldom did he fail!
It was hard to see the Grade in snow and through the failing light, so he used to take some whiskey with him, to help him with his sight.
The wind did moan and howl and tried to knock him down,
But Carson people used to cheer when Monk rode into town.

9) Earthquake and Steamers
(*From Disaster to Triumph*)

Immediately after the 1906 San Francisco earthquake, someone erected a sign close to the Ferry Building at the end of Market Street. "Things could be worse. Tomorrow you could be living in Oakland!"

Even in the midst of tragedy there were other amusing stories. Not least of which involved Enrico Caruso, the famous Italian opera singer.

Enrico Caruso was the Elvis Presley of his day. He was staying at the San Francisco's Palace Hotel at the time of the earthquake. Many victims remembered Caruso bursting into song while walking (or stumbling) through and over debris. Many thought it was morale-boosting stuff, but apparently the singer was fearful that the dust would cause permanent damage to his vocal chords. Convinced he was losing his voice, he would suddenly launch into an aria or two.

In March 1872, the small community of Lone Pine was rocked by a strong earthquake. The quake was felt throughout the Tahoe region. It was reported that some of the pass roads were visibly higher by several feet by nature rolling over on its side. Only seven structures were left standing out of the original fifty-nine in Lone Pine. Pictures were shaken off the walls in Sacramento, and thousands fled the silver mines of Virginia City. Naturalist John Muir, who was camping in

Yosemite at the time, declared it to be the most "noble" of earthquakes! The earthquake is quite often referred to as the Owens Valley Earthquake.

In June 1896, the 168-foot Steamer Ship *Tahoe* was launched at Glenbrook. She would be the longest steamer to ever operate on the lake. She was not built for the lumber industry, she was built for pleasure cruising. But she would also deliver the mail around the lakeside communities for several years. She had two wood-burning boilers, cut crystal, brass fixtures and was furnished throughout in both oak and mahogany. She had a gentleman's smoking saloon and hot and cold water in the public restrooms. The Captain for the first twenty-one years of the SS *Tahoe* (featured in the story "From Disaster to Triumph") was Ernie J. Pomin. The Pomin family has been at Tahoe City since its very first days.

When the narrow-gauge railroad joined Tahoe City to the Transcontinental Railroad, Duane Bliss closed the Carson Tahoe Lumber and Fluming Company and moved his operations over to Tahoe City. The steamers *Tahoe* and *Meteor* and the railroad now operated under the Lake Tahoe Railroad and Transportation Company. In 1901, The Tahoe Tavern Hotel opened just south of Tahoe City. A pier with an extension of the railroad track was built in conjunction with the hotel. The lavish hotel and pier were now the focal point and starting point for the new traveling tourist. In 1896, the Bliss family also acquired the SS *Tallac* from "Lucky" E.J Baldwin and renamed it the SS *Nevada*. The Bliss family had moved successfully from the old century of timber cutting to the new century of tourism. They owned one of the best hotels and the three biggest steamers on the lake.

Postscripts

1) Inside the Gatekeeper's Museum, just on the south side of Fanny Bridge by the Tahoe City dam, you'll see a written testimonial to Captain Pomin, by the members of the board of the Lake Tahoe Railroad and Transportation Company, at the time of his death in 1919.

2) Tahoe's first ever casino was built on the California side of the lake. Lucky Baldwin owned the luxurious Tallac House on Tahoe's southwest shore. It had a casino, a bowling alley, and a ballroom mounted on springs. Actor and director Eric Von Stronheim worked as a guide for the hotel, leading hiking trips up to the top of Mount Tallac, before he went to Hollywood.

3) Lucky Baldwin received his nickname for his seemingly good fortune. He had invested in a silver mine and while traveling abroad he wrote his agent to sell the worthless stock. His agent never received the letter, so the stock was never sold. Before Baldwin's return to America a silver vein was struck and the stock price rocketed. He went onto the build the Santa Anita racetrack and owned four winners of the American Derby.

4) It was Duane Leroy Bliss's fourth child, architect Walter Danforth Bliss, who designed the Tahoe Tavern Hotel in Tahoe City. He and his partner William Baker Faville designed the Saint Francis Hotel in San Francisco, which opened in 1904.

5) Ceremoniously, the *SS Meteor* was sunk in the middle of the lake on April 21, 1939. The same fate came to the Queen of the Lake, the *SS Tahoe* on August 29, 1940. William Seth Bliss (Duane Leroy's oldest son), well into his sev-

enties, thought it better to sink the proud steamers than to see them rust away on dry land.

6) The *SS Tahoe* was meant to be sunk in a hundred feet of water off Glenbrook Bay, but due a miscalculation it ended up sinking to a depth of four hundred feet.

10) The Stars of Lake Tahoe (*Mutiny at the Inn*)

There is some poetic license taken in the story "Mutiny at the Inn."

Charlie Chaplin did film the opening sequences of his 1925 film "*The Gold Rush*" above Truckee, somewhere around the present-day Boreal Ski Area. Gable starred with Loretta Young in "*Call of the Wild*," partially filmed at Lake Tahoe during the winter of 1934-35. It's possible that during this time Gable first came to the Glenbrook Inn. Returning often, he was known to help out and wait-table when the Inn was shorthanded.

The photograph shown in this book is of Clark Gable on Glenbrook beach in 1951. The love of Gable's life, Carole Lombard, came to Tahoe in 1933 to gain state residency, so she could divorce William Powell (*The Thin Man*). Gable and Lombard started their romance in 1935, at the time Gable was still married to his second wife. Many movie stars came to Nevada so that they could take advantage of the state's simplified laws governing divorce. After a short period of six weeks, they could achieve state residency, and as Nevada residents they could avail themselves of a quick divorce at the Reno courthouse.

Many big named stars have either appeared in films shot on location around Lake Tahoe or appeared in cabaret at the south shore casinos. Some have stayed awhile, too. Frank Sinatra went so far as to purchase the CalNeva Lodge on Tahoe's northern state line in the early 1960s. Marilyn Monroe was a guest at the CalNeva shortly before her death in 1962. Rita Hayworth played golf at Glenbrook while staying there in order to divorce Prince Aly. She also lived awhile in Crystal Bay with her fourth husband Dick Haymes.

Rex Bell was a Hollywood actor in 1930s known for his roles in Westerns, usually wearing one of those oversized cowboy hats. He was in a film called *"Lightnin"* filmed at the lake in 1930. The main star of the film was the comedian, humorist, and philosopher Will Rogers. Bell and Rogers were staying at the Tahoe Tavern at Tahoe City during the film. Rex's previous film had been *Loyal to the Navy* in which he starred along-side the original "It" girl Clara Bow. Bell and Bow had started a relationship following the film. While Bell was at the Tahoe Tavern, Clara came up for a visit. Rogers had never met Clara Bow before and wanted to take the young couple out to dinner.

Will Rogers suggested dinner at the CalNeva Lodge. After dinner, Rogers went to lose a dollar or two at the gaming tables. New to gambling, Clara decided to chance her luck; she signed a chit for a few chips and went to the blackjack table. Not sure of what she was doing, she ended up losing 139 chips. She was not too perturbed because she believed one chip to be worth only fifty cents. However, when the chit was presented for payment to her bank in Los Angeles, it was discovered that the chips were worth a hundred dollars apiece. In reality, she had lost nearly $14,000. Clara put a stop to the chit's payment. The matter was decided in court but it supplied Will Rogers with some good material for his one-man show. Clara Bow might just be the reason why casinos are required to have chips with their value clearly shown. Clara and Rex were married in 1931, and Bell was elected as Nevada's lieutenant governor in 1954 (re-elected in 1958).

Marilyn Monroe and Clark Gable appeared together in what proved to be the last film for either star "*The Misfits.*" The film was about the wrangling of wild mustangs, and it was filmed in and around Reno. Not a hugely successful film, the two stars turned in their best performances. Co-starring with them was Montgomery Clift. A decade earlier, Montgomery Clift played the troubled young man in a tragic love triangle with Shelly Winters and a gorgeous young Elizabeth Taylor. The film "*A Place in the Sun,*" was filmed around Lake Tahoe's southwest shore and featured Cascade Lake as the spot where Shelly Winter's character drowned (or was murdered?).

Cascade Lake is just over the ridge from Emerald Bay, (the setting for the "Three-Toed Island" story). It was at Emerald Bay that an attractive Jeanette MacDonald and Nelson Eddy sang their "Indian Love Call." The film "*Rose Marie*" also featured two future Oscar winners just embarking on their careers: a young James Stewart and a young David Niven. James Stewart played Jeanette MacDonald's young fugitive brother and David Niven played MacDonald's unrequited young suitor. Forty years later it was a much older James Stewart who starred with John Wayne in what was to be the Duke's last film, "*The Shootist,*" filmed in Carson City and Genoa.

Another featured murder here at Lake Tahoe, was the murder of Michael Corleone's brother Fredo. Shot while fishing from a small boat, Fredo's body was dropped over the side and it went straight to the bottom. Had the Mafia learned earlier that dead bodies don't float in Lake Tahoe; they could have saved a lot of money on concrete shoes. The Henry J. Kaiser estate at Tahoe Pines served as the Corleone's Tahoe property in "*The Godfather Part ll.*" Although the main house was replaced by deluxe condominiums a few years ago, the boat house featured in the film is still there. (If you have watched the film and are able to identify the murderer you could possibly run the risk of keeping Fredo company.)

Author's note: I was a young man living in South Africa when I saw the second *Godfather* film. I knew nothing about Tahoe at the time. Twenty-five years later I returned to South Africa, and while driving around Hout Bay close to Cape Town, I saw a small café called "Tahoe's Coffee Shop." A couple named Dave and Leian had opened the café after they were married at Lake Tahoe a few months earlier. The groom's family was from my hometown in England.

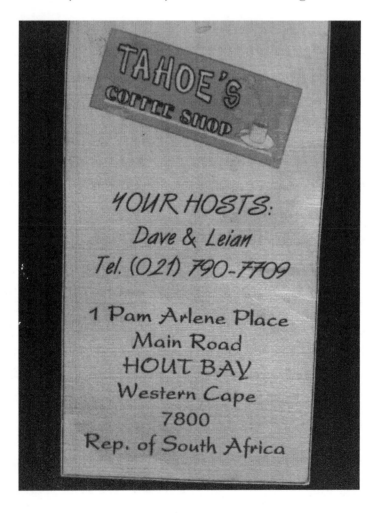

Postscripts

1) The same year as "*The Gold Rush,*" Charlie Chaplin supposedly entered a Charlie Chaplin look-a-like contest and won third place.

2) While staying at Lake Tahoe in the summer of 1933, Carole Lombard cut the ribbon to officially open Highway 28 along Tahoe's northeast shore. With this last section opened, it was finally possible to drive right around the lake.

3) Unlike other celebrities who usually went to Reno, Carole Lombard obtained her divorce from William Powell at the Carson City courthouse. Despite the divorce, the couple remained friends and starred in the film *"My Man Godfrey"* in 1936.

4) While gaining her Nevada residency, Carole Lombard stayed with her good friend Mary Stack. Mary's son Robert developed a teenage crush for the blond starlet. In 1942, Robert had a small part in Carole Lombard's last film *"To Be or Not To Be."* He achieved fame as Eliot Ness in TV's *"The Untouchables."*

5) Although Jeanette MacDonald was two years older than Clara Bow, Clara was a star of silent movies and Jeanette was a singing star of the talkies. Jeanette MacDonald's only other film in 1936 was *"San Francisco,"* which co-starred Clark Gable. It was arguably her best performance. Clark Gable said of Jeanette MacDonald, "All I do is shut up and listen to her sing!" The following year she starred in *"Firefly"* with Allan Jones (Jones was also in *"Rose Marie"*).

6) Ironically, "*The Misfits*" was also the last film for Rex Bell.

7) Despite being contemporaries and going on to make more than seventy films apiece. Jimmy Stewart and David Niven never appeared in the same film again.

11) The Squaw Valley Olympics 1960 (In the Halls of Zeus)

They talk of the two miracles of Squaw Valley: the first was the weather, and the second being the victory of the US hockey team.

Although there had been little by the way of snow in the Sierras during December 1959. January 1960 was much better and things looked good. But the following month brought warmer weather. For the first two weeks of February, it only rained at elevations below 8500 feet. One week before the Games, the continuous rain had melted a large part of the valley snow pack, puddles formed everywhere, and Squaw Creek was overflowing. There was a chance, if it stopped raining, that they could bring snow down from the higher elevations and replace what had been washed away, but things were looking bleak. The contingency plan to hold some of the ski races at Slide Mountain became a distinct possibility.

Fortunately, with only four days left, a cold front came through and produced three and a half feet of new snow. It seemed like a godsend but the cold front was slow moving. On the morning of the opening ceremonies, a blizzard was blowing through the valley. A major problem was facing the first exclusively televised Winter Games. Visibility was down to zero and the cameras could see nothing! Another foot of snow fell that morning, and traffic getting to Squaw had major problems. Vice President Richard Nixon was supposed to arrive by helicopter, but the weather was considered too dangerous. With Nixon delayed, the ceremonies had to be pushed back. Nixon arrived an hour late, and as he made his way to the microphone to declare the Games open, the skies cleared and the wind died down...... which made the Soviets think that the Americans had discovered some form of climate control. As Walt Disney (the master of ceremonies) released two thousand doves, the scene was bathed in sunshine.

Before 1960, the American ice hockey team had never won a gold medal. For years the Canadians had dominated the sport, until the Soviets won gold in Cortina in 1956. In 1960 the American team was on paper the weakest team they had ever fielded. They were not expected to win a medal of any color. They had lost four times to college teams in their warm-up matches and, just thirteen days before the games, had been easily beaten by the Soviets. The American coach Jack Riley was still making changes to the team up to the last minute. It was meant to be a battle between the two powerhouses, the Canadians and the Soviets, at which the Americans would be spectators and cheering on the Canadians.

There were nine teams, split into three groups, and the top two teams of each group progressed to the championship round. The six teams who advanced would all then play each other, and the gold would go to the team with the best record. The Canadians had three of the top five goal scorers on their team, and leading up to their match against the US they had never scored less than four goals. In the game against Canada, the American goalie Jack McCartan stopped thirty-nine shots out of forty and team USA pulled off a massive upset, winning 2-1. Against the Soviets, the Americans were down 2-3 after the second period. The US scored the only two goals of the third and won 4-3. The feat of winning the gold in 1960 was perhaps, overshadowed in 1980 by the victory of a younger American team, but the gold at Squaw was the country's first.

Postscripts

1) Native Americans were brought in especially to do an occasional snow dance to get the late winter started.

2) Jean Vaurnet won the downhill gold medal at Squaw, which undoubtedly helped him sell a few sunglasses.

3) The Squaw Valley Olympics were the first to have a purpose built Olympic Village for the athletes. Visiting dignitaries stayed at the Tahoe Tavern in Tahoe City; the tavern burned down in 1964.

4) It was considered an unnecessary expense to build a bob sleigh run for the small number of entrants. So despite the plans for the run, it was never built, and there were no bob sleigh events at Squaw Valley.

5) Before the third period of the Americans' final game against the Czech team, down 3-4, the US team was visited by the Soviet coach, who suggested the exhausted team take a couple of breaths of pure oxygen. It certainly didn't hurt; the Americans came out and scored six times in the final period to run-out 9 – 4 victors.

Squaw Valley's Blyth Arena, location of the USA's first ever Gold Medal for Ice Hockey (photo shows figure skater.) In 1983 the roof collapse and the arena was subsequently demolished.

12) Snowshoe Thompson (Sesquicentennial)

So many stories have been written about the heroic Norwegian that little can be added. Just before Thompson died, in 1876, Dan De Quille, Mark Twain's mentor at *The Territorial Enterprise,* interviewed the remarkable mailman. De Quille wrote an article for the Overland Monthly, which did not appear until 1886. Still, De Quille was able to recall some of the interview and give us some first-hand knowledge of this extraordinary man.

Thompson described to De Quille how, during one of his mail expeditions, he came upon a pack of timber-wolves. The wolves were in the middle of devouring the corpse of a mule deer. He said it was the only time he might have wished for a gun. Because of the slope of the hill, he was unable to avoid skiing straight past the pack. One of the wolves noticed him on his approach and stopped eating. This wolf then sat in a position facing Thompson, and broke out in to the most mournful of howls! The first wolf was then joined by all the others, seated in a row, and all of them howled as Thompson hurriedly skied by. He could hear their plaintive howling for several minutes, but fortunately none of them pursued him.

From De Quille's article we also learn that our Norwegian hero was one of the twenty-nine survivors at the First Battle of Pyramid Lake in May of 1860. Thompson recounted his narrow brush with death. (We have to assume that our hero was armed on this occasion.) With his own horse shot out from underneath him, the Norwegian fled the Paiute Indians on foot. One of his mounted comrades is then supposed to have shouted, "Why don't you mount the horse behind you?" At which time Thompson turned around and brushed the soft nose of a rider-less horse that had been right behind him all the time. Mounting the horse, he made good his escape. Thompson claimed it was the hand of the Lord.

By every known account, Thompson was a good man, and what he achieved defies any reasonable assessment of what a good man does. He delivered the mail twice a month over twenty Sierra winters. It has to be remembered that people living on the eastern side of the Sierra, in the years before the railroad, were isolated by the whims of Mother Nature. An annual four hundred inches of snow on the higher ridges is but a normal winter in the Sierras. The snow was like an impenetrable wall without a door; people on the eastern side of the Sierras were cut off for weeks at a time. Thompson delivered much needed medicine to people who would have otherwise gone without. He helped all those he came across and also rescued a few lost individuals. A devout Christian, he carried his Bible throughout his journeys.

He did seek recompense for his services from the United States Postal, Service in 1872, by which time he was able to take advantage of the Transcontinental Railroad for a journey east to Washington, D.C. Those that heard Thompson's tale were agreed that he should be compensated. But empathetic as they were, Thompson was never paid by the United States Postal Service! It is a debt that the US government still has not paid. Any normal man might have felt ill-used, but not Snowshoe Thompson. Forgotten by those who owed him the most, he was not forgotten for his many kindnesses to ordinary people. Thompson was paid small amounts of money by individuals for deliveries of personal items and necessities. Although not paid by the Postal Service, he still continued to deliver the US Mail over the mountains for another four years!

In May of 1876, while planting seed on his ranch near Markleeville in California, it is believed Thompson's appendix ruptured, and this famous son of the Sierra died two days later, at the age of forty-nine. He was to reach Genoa, his long-time postal destination, one final time, and he was buried in the town's small cemetery. Remembered by so many, there are statues to this fearless man throughout the Sierra, and on his grave in the Genoa cemetery there are three plaques. The plaque nearest to the headstone reads:

"AS A TRIBUTE TO A GREAT COMPATRIOT FROM TELEMARK THIS PLAQUE WAS PRESENTED BY THE NORWEGIAN OLYMPIC SKI TEAM COMPETING AT SQUAW VALLEY IN FEBRUARY 1960."

Postscripts

1) Once familiar with the terrain, Thompson's preference was to travel by night and navigate by the stars. On cloudy nights he took note of the thickest lichen growing on the north facing side of the pine trees. He added to his knowledge by making mental notes of significant rock formations and streams. Years later Thompson stated he had never been lost in the mountains.

2) Thompson is well remembered for having saved the life of James Sisson. Thompson found Sisson snowbound in his remote cabin, suffering from severe frostbite and unable to

walk. Thompson made a fire and stacked enough wood to keep Sisson warm while he went on to Genoa for help. Sisson had to have both legs amputated. The doctor had no chloroform, so Thompson had to go to Sacramento to get some. In saving Sisson's life, Thompson traveled four hundred miles.

3) Born Jon Tostensen, his named was Americanized to John Thompson. However, on his grave his name is misspelled as John Thomson.

4) Singer Johnny Horton (*Battle of New Orleans*) wrote a song in tribute to Snowshoe Thompson, sung with banjo accompaniment, it is very similar in style to the theme tune of the "*Beverly Hillbillies*" TV series.

5) Singer Tennessee Ernie Ford (*Sixteen Tons*) also recorded a tribute song. Ford's song is completely different to the Horton song, but both songs are called "Snow Shoe Thompson."

35170032R00148

Made in the USA
San Bernardino, CA
16 June 2016